ESSENTIAL HUNA

DISCOVERING AND INTEGRATING YOUR THREE SELVES

Arlyn J. Macdonald

INFINITY PUBLISHING

Inner Power and Light Company
62880 W. La Salle Road, #180
Montrose, CO 81401
www.huna.us

ISBN 0-7414-1373-6

Published by:

INFINITY
PUBLISHING.COM

519 West Lancaster Avenue
Haverford, PA 19041-1413
Info@buybooksontheweb.com
www.buybooksontheweb.com
Toll-free (877) BUY BOOK
Local Phone (610) 520-2500
Fax (610) 519-0261

Printed in the United States of America

Printed on Recycled Paper

Published April 2003

Dedication

This book is dedicated first to my dear Little Sister, my own *'Unihipili*, who shares the challenges of living with me and who has inwardly made known to me, in so many ways, the rightness of the Huna principles. She is my constant and true companion and I acknowledge her part in all we accomplish. I dedicate this book also to my *'Aumakua*, whose Divine Guidance, Wisdom and Presence fills me with inspiration and creativity. I am so very grateful for the love and devotion of both my other Selves.

I also dedicate this work to my loving husband, Donald, who has been and is my strength and my fellow Huna student for the past 30 years. His dedication to this project is a reflection of his love for Huna and for service to his fellow travelers.

And, lastly, I dedicate this book to Max Freedom Long, whose life's research kept the Huna truths from being lost to the world forever.

TABLE OF CONTENTS

INTRODUCTION

The Truth appears to us in many forms. We don't know the Truth with our five physical senses, rather we recognize it with our hearts and with our minds. It is an inner knowing. Our ancient ancestors knew the Truth. They knew that God was a personal God. They knew that we are connected to all things, that there is a unity to life beyond our physical perceptions.

Archaeologists and related scientists misinterpreted many ancient belief systems, based on their own limited understanding of God. What may have seemed primitive on the surface were, in reality, highly sophisticated spiritual belief systems, often more sophisticated than many of our present beliefs. The understanding today of the spiritual depths of the Native American beliefs, which were once labeled superstition, is a prime example of how personal opinions color the Truth.

This misinterpretation also occurred in the Hawai'ian Islands. Here Western European thinking and the convictions of the American Christian missionaries influenced the perceptions of the spiritual beliefs of the native Hawai'ian. The Truths of this ancient system were nearly lost. That would have been devastating to the world. For the teachings of the ancient Hawai'ian, I believe, explain more clearly and have more practical application to our current personal and spiritual growth than any other religion or belief system.

These teachings are called "***Huna***," the Hawai'ian word that means "secret," by Max Freedom Long. Max Long, an American, spent his life researching the concepts and reconstructing the applications of the teachings. He developed a Western understanding of these secret Hawaiian principles. His work continues today under the leadership of many dedicated people. "***Huna*** is neither a completed body of knowledge nor a static theory," according to John Bainbridge, in his book, *Huna Magic*. The study of ***Huna*** is an on-going search into the practical application of the psychology-religion-philosophy system of the ancient Hawai'ians by each individual who uses it.

The complete spiritual life of the ancient Hawai'ian will never be known. Much of their lore, history and beliefs sadly will never be recovered. This system was a secret system taught only to the inner circle of priests, royalty and chiefs in Hawai'i. It was not taught to the lower classes, unless an individual showed extraordinary talent.

The Hawai'ian people had no word for religion, for all of life was sacred, holy and connected, and was to be respected and honored. The principles of the system were the way of life for the people. The physical world and the world of spirit were equally important and accessible. Every plant, animal, person, and spirit was loved and honored and the abundance of nature was gladly shared with everyone. The Hawai'ian perspective of life teaches us many things.

The practice of ***Huna*** does not interfere with any other belief or religion. It actually explains many of the mysteries of the other teachings, for Long in his research discovered that there are traces or remnants of ***Huna*** in most of the ancient spiritual teachings found throughout the world.

This particular study of ***Huna*** uses exercises, which I call inneractivities. "**Inner**" is defined in *The Merriam Webster Dictionary* as "near a center, especially of influence" and "of or relating to the mind or spirit." "**Active**" is defined as "causing or involving action or change." **Inneractivities** are therefore defined as **"an influencing process that causes change near the center of your spirit/mind."**

Words are symbols for concepts. Many teachings use secret language or employ sacred symbols to describe the principles of the system. I use the Hawai'ian words and symbols, whenever applicable, to describe the various parts of the ***Huna*** knowledge. The Hawai'ian words more clearly define and describe the principles of this knowledge because of the structure and meanings of that language.

Remember that we are whole beings.
Any divisions or words used to describe separateness are simply for the convenience of understanding. They are in reality only illusions and not the true nature of our being.
We are more than the sum total of all our parts.

WE ARE WHOLE AND DIVINE.

In using these ***Huna*** teachings, we are not attempting to become Hawai'ian, or to become a *Kahuna* (a native priest), or to consider ourselves different from who and what we are. These teachings are from the Western perspective of the understanding of the ancient Hawai'ian concepts and principles. I have synthesized the knowledge of ***Huna*** with other systems that I believe are ***Huna*** in essence, which may be helpful in your understanding of the principles.

The ***Huna*** teachings were once spread around the known world in our ancient past. We now reclaim the rich heritage of their spiritual understanding and the practical application of the knowledge for our present life. By understanding and practicing the ***Huna*** teachings, we take our rightful place in the process of creation. We pledge to live the hurtless and helpful life. And we take full responsibility for creating our own prosperous and healthy future and the future of the world.

May the Light of your own *'Aumakua* illuminate your understanding of these teachings,

-- Arlyn J. Macdonald

USE OF THIS WORKBOOK

This workbook is based on the discoveries of Max Freedom Long and the other learned men and women whose concepts are ***Huna*** in essence. It is designed to facilitate the understanding of some of the concepts and beliefs of the ancient peoples of Hawai'i as reconstructed and interpreted by Long. ***Huna*** is a practical and workable philosophy of living that can be used successfully by everyone.

The workbook is divided into sections. Each section is followed by a specific **Inneractivity** to illustrate the teachings and to help you learn how to communicate with your three Selves. The communication between the Selves is vital to your personal and spiritual growth. The **Inneractivities** help you become more fully aware of the great potentials that are largely untapped within you. Space has been added for your personal comments after each **Inneractivity**. In addition, **Continuing Inneractivities** have been included so that, instead of putting this book on your shelf, you continue to use it in your process of self-discovery.

As with any theory or working method, certain assumptions must be made in order to understand the model. You may question some of the ideas at first, but keep in mind that the words are only symbols for the Truth concepts behind the words. The Truths in ***Huna*** are the same universal Truths taught in a slightly different, but ultimately more practical and complete way.

SIMPLE GUIDE TO PRONOUNCING THE HAWAI'IAN LANGUAGE

The vowels always have the same sound:

A as in **a**rm, **E** as in ob**e**y, **I** as in mach**i**ne, **O** as in **o**ld, **U** as in m**oo**n.

The accent falls on the first syllable in words of two syllables, such as po-oh (po'-oh). In words of more than two syllables, the accent falls on the second to the last syllable (the penult), such as aloha (a-lo'-ha). Some words have their syllables marked, such as ka'-na-ka.

HISTORY OF POLYNESIA AND HAWAI'I

14,000 years ago the ancient peoples of the South Pacific were sailing their double-hulled canoes between the islands of Polynesia, which stretched from New Zealand to the Hawai'ian Islands to Easter Island, covering a great triangle of 2,000 miles. This Pacific triangle was explored, settled and had regular trade between the Maori, Samoans, Tongans, Tahitians, Marquesans, Hawai'ians and Easter Islanders for thousands of years before Columbus ever set sail for the New World across the Atlantic Ocean.

The Polynesians had sophisticated and highly evolved cultures, which were completely misunderstood by the early European explorers, who "discovered" the islands, and later by the Christian missionaries who came to "save" the souls of the natives. These native cultures were not technologically advanced as were the Europeans, but they were highly advanced in the areas of ecology, understanding human consciousness, the use of energy, and the process of healing.

No one knows from where the Polynesian people originated or the route they took to get to their island homes. Some anthropologists speculate that the people came from the Arab lands passing through India following the great Chaldeo-Arabian commerce routes. These people are said to have occupied the Asiatic archipelago from Sumatra to Luzon and Timor before setting sail for the South Pacific.

Other scientists, including Thor Heyerdahl of *Kon-Tiki* fame, believe the Polynesian people came from South America. Max Freedom Long, who recovered much of the ***Huna*** system, concluded from his research that the Polynesians originated in the Sahara Desert when it was lush and fertile. The people moved into the Valley of the Nile as the rivers in their own land dried up. They helped the ancient Egyptians build the pyramids with their understanding of energy. According to Long, the ancient priests foresaw the future of a coming "intellectual" darkness in Egypt, a time when the sacred teachings were in danger of being lost. They also foresaw an uninhabited land where they could go to preserve the knowledge. The twelve tribes that made up these ancient peoples gathered and began their long journey through India and eastward, to the isolation of the Islands of Hawai'i -- the land of the prophecy.

Still other scientists believe that the Polynesian people came from a great island in the Pacific Ocean that sank - the land called Mu or Lemuria. There are stories of this great land of Mu, the Motherland, among the legends of the various Polynesian islands and also among other ancient cultures.

There is also a story that tells of Star People, who came from the star system called the Pleiades long before the rise of Atlantis.

These Star people settled on the continent of Mu and traveled widely throughout the world sharing their knowledge with selected groups of people in different lands. The people of Mu were very small in stature, but full of wisdom. When Mu broke up and sank, the Mu travelers were stranded. Many cultures around the world have legends of the "Little People," including Hawaiʻi, where they are called the *Menehune* or the *Mu,* meaning *"people of the secret power."* James Churchward, noted archaeologist, believes that Mu was settled over 50,000 years ago and that the people who inhabit the earth today are all descendants of the people of Mu.

Another story tells of the *Maoli* or "the ancient ones" who came to the Islands of Hawaiʻi to settle. Their descendants were conquered in the mid-twelfth century by the Polynesian invaders from Tahiti, who imposed their *kapu* (taboo) system on the *Maoli*. The *Maoli* were also called the *Mu.*

Pali Jae Lee and Koko Willis, co-authors of *Tales from the Night Rainbow*, report on the most current theory, based on carbon dating Pacific Basin artifacts and home sites. They cite Anthropologist Patrick Kirch, who did his work at the University of California, Berkeley. He postulates that the Proto-Polynesian peoples (those who became the Polynesian race) were nomads who lived totally on the sea, depending on the sea for all their needs. These people he believes came from several different places bringing their own cultures with them. Many came from China and India. The people who became the natives of Mexico and North America were part of this group. The Proto-Tongic group was the first group to break away around 3500 B.C. and settle in one specific area. 500 years later the first people settled in Hawaiʻi.

Remains of an ancient Polynesian skeleton have recently been uncovered in the Channel Islands off the coast of California. Kennewick Man discovered in Oregon is believed to be Polynesian. The ancient tribe of Japan, the Ainu, is also believed to be of Polynesian origin. British Columbia and Alaska have remnants of Polynesian culture, giving more credence to the oceanic nomad theory.

The ancient Hawaiʻian, in their most sacred chants, preserved records that the Polynesians came from a land which the missionaries translated as "Tahiti." No amount of explaining could convince the missionaries that the Tahiti the Hawaiʻian were describing was a dimension of the spiritual plane, not the other Polynesian island by the same name. The best explanation understood by the missionaries was that the Hawaiʻian said they had descended from the land of the gods.

The Hawaiʻian Islands are located 2,000 miles southwest of California in the middle of the Pacific Ocean. There are 132 islands in the 1,600-mile long chain, but only 7 of the main 8 islands are inhabited. The remoteness of the islands of Hawaiʻi made possible the preservation of the **"secret"** teachings. The Hawaiʻian islands were visited by the Spanish in the 16th century and later by the

Portuguese. King Kamehameha I, who united the Islands of Hawai'i under one rule, is rumored to have confiscated a great silver treasure from these early visitors and this treasure is said to be buried with him in his secret tomb.

It wasn't until Captain James Cook anchored off the island of Kaua'i in 1778 that the Hawai'ian Islands became well known in Europe and America. By the time Captain Cook arrived, the Hawai'ian had long since ended their great voyages and had become quite isolated from their neighbors. When Captain Cook found the island of Kaua'i, he thought he had discovered a primitive paradise. He didn't realize he had stumbled onto an advanced civilization that had been isolated for 600 years. That isolation had spawned corruption in the islands. Cook's arrival spurred the overthrow of the government **and** the overthrow of the basic religious life of the people, including the *taboo* or *kapu* system. The *kapu* system was a complicated system of restrictions, permissions and prohibitions designed to keep the common people in obedience to the chiefs and the priests.

The loss of their central belief system, together with the promised riches of the new whaling industry and the spreading of deadly European diseases, devastated the traditional Hawai'ian way of life. Thus, conditions were ripe for the American missionaries from the Congregational Church in Boston to take over the religious life of the Hawa'ian, converting many native people to Christianity, and pressuring the government to outlaw the *Kahuna* (the native priests) and their seemingly "magical" practices.

The Western European mind was not open to the island practices that appeared to be sorcery or magic. The native *Kahuna* could heal broken bones instantly, revive people who had drowned, call the turtles and the sharks, and change the weather. They had the knowledge of all the medicinal plants of the islands and were great healers. They could also walk across fiery lava beds and not get burned. They could see into and change the future. Most threatening to the missionaries was the ability of the *Kahuna* to pray someone to death. This is the primary reason the missionaries were so afraid of the *Kahuna*, for in the Christian belief system all "magic" came from the devil and was evil.

The missionaries gained influence with the rulers of Hawai'i and soon the *Kahuna* were outlawed. Their practices were made illegal and they were subject to imprisonment and fines. The *Kahuna* continued to practice in secret and it became more difficult for foreigners to find out anything about them or their beliefs. (The *Kahuna* practiced openly, and without prosecution, after 1978 with the passage of the American Indian Religious Freedom Act by Congress.)

The missionaries set about immediately to write down the Hawai'ian language. Before their arrival it was only an oral language. The missionaries devised an alphabet and compiled a dictionary. They began to teach English to the Hawaiians, who had a great enthusiasm and respect for learning. All the chiefs and commoners soon learned how to read and write in English. Much of the Hawai'ian knowledge that has been preserved comes from this period.

From the time of King Kamehameha I, who succeeded in uniting the Islands of Hawaiʻi in 1796 to the raising of the American flag over the islands in 1898, Western thought, cultural pressure, technology, and diseases influenced and changed the lives of the Hawaiʻian people. Before the arrival of the white European in the middle of the 19th century there were 400,000 people living in Hawaiʻi. Today, approximately 12,000 people of pure Hawaiʻian ancestry remain. In recent years, there has been a great movement in the Islands to reclaim the culture and language of Hawaii.

As knowledge of the Hawaiʻian Islands and its rich resources were exploited, other cultures were brought to the islands as laborers and intermarried with the original Hawaiʻian people. The acceptance and integration of these other cultures by the island people create a unique society that significantly affects the rest of the world.

Hawaiʻi has not only become a world vacation paradise, but more importantly:

Hawaiʻi has become a model for a culturally diverse global community!

HISTORY OF *HUNA*

Huna, is the Hawaiʻian word for *"secret."* It is the name given to the secret body of knowledge of the ancient *Kahuna* by Max Freedom Long, who uncovered and reconstructed the main elements of the ancient psychological - religious - philosophical system of the Hawaiʻian people. The priests of the Islands of Hawaiʻi were called ***Kahuna***, which means the *"keepers, guardians or transmitters of the secret."*

> *HUNA* MEANS "SECRET."
>
> *KAHUNA* MEANS "GUARDIAN OR TRANSMITTER OF THE SECRET."

The Hawaiʻian language and the other Polynesian dialects were oral languages, that is, there were no written symbols or alphabets for the language. All knowledge was handed down from one generation to the next orally. Meticulous care was taken to pass on the precise knowledge and words. The Christian missionaries created an alphabet for the Hawaiʻian language and began to write down the language in order to translate the *Bible* into Hawaiʻian using their best guess as to letters and sounds. This also happened in other Polynesian islands and that is why we have different letters and sounds for the same words among the islands.

Unfortunately, the concepts of the Hawaiʻian spiritual beliefs were difficult to translate into English. The missionaries did not fully understand what the Hawaiʻians were trying to describe. So the missionaries translated the misunderstood Hawaiʻian beliefs and spiritual concepts into their own Christian model and made little attempt to understand the true beliefs of the people. These problems, and the lack of understanding of each language by the other culture, created many false or incomplete translations of words, ideas and concepts. However, without the work of the Christian missionaries the culture and knowledge of the ancient Hawaiʻian would not be as well preserved as it is today.

THE KAHUNA

There were many kinds of *Kahuna*. They were the educated professionals, the doctors, lawyers, architects, scientists, priests, educators, counselors to chiefs and kings, agriculturalists, master artisans and master craftsmen of their time. The term meant the highest expert in his or her field. There were over 40 kinds of craft *Kahuna* and 14 *Kahuna* of the healing arts. Much of the knowledge of the ancient *Kahuna* was far more advanced than our knowledge today. Their knowledge of the use of medicinal plants is one example. The *Kahuna* were great healers and were even able to arrest cancer and heart trouble. They also knew more about human psychology than we understand with our current theories. The term *Kahuna* began to be misused in the mid-1800's by foreigners who didn't understand Hawai'ian. By 1900, most foreigners believed the term *Kahuna* meant an evil sorcerer.

MAX FREEDOM LONG

Max Long came to the Hawai'ian Islands in 1917 to be a teacher in a plantation school on the Island of Hawai'i. He spent his boyhood in Wyoming and graduated from U.C.L.A. with a degree in education. He worked as a photographer and gold mine assayer. It was just by coincidence that he happened to come to Hawai'i at all.

It wasn't long before Max became interested in the seemingly magical and miraculous events that were part of the Hawai'ian life around him. He tried to find out the secret behind the "miracles," but the Hawai'ians wouldn't answer his many questions. He stopped asking questions then and began listening. He listened for three years and carefully recorded what he heard, but still he had no answer. In frustration he decided to return to the States, but was reluctant to go until he discovered what was behind the magic.

He went to the island of O'ahu and was told that the Bishop Museum might hold the answers. According to Long's account, he went to the museum and was shown to the office of Dr. William Tufts Brigham. Dr. Brigham just retired as Curator of the Bishop Museum and was a distinguished botanist and geologist from Harvard University. Dr. Brigham's interest had turned in his later years toward ethnology (the science dealing with the races of human beings, their origins, distribution, characteristics and relations). He spent the last forty years of his life privately studying and researching similar tales of magic. He even walked across burning lava under the protection of two *Kahuna* and experienced telepathic prayer and healing. During his work with the Bishop Museum, Dr. Brigham headed a party into a Hawai'ian burial cave that yielded what is believed to be the most valuable single assortment of relics ever found in a cave, including a large assortment of the rarest Hawai'ian calabashes. He was recognized around the world for his scientific abilities.

Dr. Brigham was impressed with Max Long and interviewed him about his personal beliefs, what he had read, and the nature of his research into the question of *Kahuna* magic. They became friends and in 1921, Dr. Brigham turned his forty years of research notes over to Long, whom he had selected to carry on the search. He encouraged Long to continue until he found the answers to how the magic worked.

LOOK FOR....
*A CONSCIOUSNESS
*A FORCE
*A SUBSTANCE THROUGH WHICH THE FORCE ACTS

.....DR. BRIGHAM'S ELEMENTS OF A "MIRACLE"

He taught him more about the scientific method of research and instructed him to look for three things that would explain the "miracles" of the *Kahuna*: a consciousness, a force, and a substance through which the force acted. Dr. Brigham felt that if one of these elements could be found, it would lead to the others.

Dr. Brigham was not the only scientist searching for the answers. Many people were trying to learn about the great body of secret knowledge, scientists and laymen alike. Since the *Kahuna* had been outlawed, it was more and more difficult to learn any information from them or about them. Only the *Kahuna* knew the secret, inner teachings; teachings of which most Hawai'ians were unaware. And it was becoming more and more difficult for the *Kahuna* to find young Hawai'ian disciples to train, who were interested in learning the secret knowledge and carrying on the traditions. As the older *Kahuna* died, their knowledge died with them.

THE KEY WAS IN THE LANGUAGE ITSELF!

Long spent several more years in Hawai'i diligently and scientifically searching for the answers. He eventually returned to the mainland disheartened. However, in 1931, in the middle of the night, an idea came to him that just might be the key. The language itself must contain the answers! The secrets were in the language, not in the everyday conversational language, but the language as used by the priests, the *Kahuna.* All the scientists had overlooked the obvious. He restarted his research looking at the coded information in the root words of the Hawai'ian language. He also researched the words and the symbols used by the *Kahuna* to describe the various aspects of the sacred teachings.

HOW THE KEY WORKED

Each word in the Hawai'ian language is made of small root words that fully describe the object or event. (For example: the word "aloha" is made up of the root words *a, lo, ha, alo,* and *loha.*) By searching for the alternative meanings of the root words or their esoteric meanings, Long recovered a great deal of knowledge about the secret system. Hawai'ian is a rich and multidimensional language and words were carefully selected for the richness of their meanings. A word could have as many as seven meanings layered one on top of the other. There were *Kahuna* who would be commissioned to select the proper name for places, temples and other important things. Each name had several meanings beginning with the outer or surface meaning and encompassing the spiritual, inner meaning. Hawai'ian words and names are considered extremely important because of the power contained in them.

What Long uncovered and reconstructed is a great treasure of beliefs that more fully explain the universe and how it works. Long spent 54 years researching and experimenting with the teachings. Before his death in 1971 he had compiled a "serviceable restoration of ***Huna***" or the secret knowledge. All of the other variations of the ***Huna*** system being taught now are based on the work of Max Freedom Long.

Long had the privilege of studying under native *Kahuna* on the Big Island of Hawai'i and experiencing first-hand the power of the *Kahuna.* His studies and his meticulous and scientific research brought the secret knowledge back to the people of Hawai'i and to the rest of the world. He wrote seven books describing his scientific research, formed a research association and corresponded with people from all over the globe, some of whom were able to add to the ***Huna*** knowledge. Long discovered this secret knowledge was not just limited to Hawai'i, but is found in the ancient teachings of many of the world religions.

The knowledge he recovered is, according to Alan P. Lewis, author of *Living in Harmony Through Kahuna Wisdom,* "in some ways more complete than the cumulative thought of modern physicists, physicians and metaphysicians." It gives us a better understanding of energy, a more complete picture of the human psyche, a method for changing the future, a detailed explanation of how to make an effective and powerful prayer, and how the healing process works through the Divine within.

RELIGION IS THE SCIENCE OF HUMANKIND IN RELATIONSHIP TO GOD.

Is ***Huna*** a religion? The definition of religion is "a belief in Higher Beings and a Supreme Being." Religion can also be defined as "the science of humankind in relationship to God." The ancient Hawai'ian believed in Higher Beings, but they had no word for their religion. It was their way of life. ***Huna*** is more than a religion, it is a way of life. It enables us to heal ourselves and others; to consciously avoid hurt; to be of helpful service to others and to the Earth; to take responsibility for creating our own lives; and, to establish a real and viable connection to our Higher Self and to God.

***HUNA* IS A WAY OF LIFE.**

BASIC BELIEFS OF THE ANCIENT HAWAI'IAN

We will never know the complete belief system of the ancient Hawai'ian, for much of it has been lost to the world, including the original language. There are few, if any, *Kahuna* or knowledgeable priests left today who know and practice the ancient "arts." Most of them prefer to practice in secret. If you were to go to Hawai'i today to try to find a *Kahuna* of the old system, it would be difficult. After the American Indian Religious Freedom Act was passed, some Kahuna came out of hiding to practice openly once more, but they are still not easy to find.

The term *"Kahuna"* originally referred to a person selected as a young child and trained in one of the various disciplines. This person became skilled in his or her particular field and was initiated by a natural or adoptive parent. It is recorded that at about age thirteen a *Kahuna* initiate could hold a piece of fragile pumice stone in the hand and after saying a "prayer" cause the stone to crumble without using physical force. Today, priests and ministers of Western religions, psychics, healers and even surfers use the term *Kahuna.* In Hawai'i, the title of *Kahuna* is given to a master, someone highly skilled and respected in his or her field.

According to Julius Scammon Rodman, author of *The Kahuna Sorcerers of Hawaii, Past and Present*, the mysterious powers of the *Kahuna* were recorded as far back as the 5th century. Rodman lists 20 different orders of religious *Kahuna*, from High Priest to black sorcerer. *Kahuna* masters of magic and prophecy dominated every level of Hawai'ian life. They were feared and respected by kings and commoners alike. High Priests were rare for they had to master all the orders. These High Priests or *Puhiokaoka* were the most spiritually developed *Kahuna* and were able to invoke the blessings of the gods for the people. Only after a lifetime of discipline, training and complex practices could these priests bridge the void between the physical and the spiritual planes. They would be considered adepts in other spiritual disciplines.

The kings were considered to have a natural link with the gods through their family lineage that began when the gods formed the world. The legends and lore of ancient Hawai'i speak of the gods and the creation of the world.

The ancient Hawaiʻian did not separate the physical world from the spiritual world. Medicine, religion and sorcery were all one in an integrated system of belief. They had a pervasive belief in the supernatural and awareness of the psychic power in themselves and in nature.

THE PHYSICAL WORLD WAS NOT SEPARATE FROM THE SPIRITUAL WORLD.

To the uninitiated native, the gods were an important part of every day life. They worshipped a pantheon of gods that was carefully ordered into a hierarchy of gods and lesser gods. There was no concept of a single "God" as taught by the Christian missionaries. Instead "God" was a very personal thing and not some intangible spirit that had to be petitioned. The ancient Hawaiʻian believed that everything had its place and everything was in its place; the world was well-ordered. Well-ordered meant that the entire Universe is a continuum. The human portion of this continuum is evolving in a well-ordered manner from a lower or beginning level to a higher or more advanced level. The rest of the Universe continuum is also evolving from lower levels to higher levels.

Another basic belief was that the human mind is unable to grasp the true nature of Ultimate God. The initiated knew that God was a triune being, Divine Father, Divine Mother and Divine Child. Between God and humankind were several grades or levels of other Conscious Beings (the gods). Because of the limited capacity of the human mind, it was difficult to understand the next level beyond humankind and therefore impossible to comprehend Ultimate God.

GOD WAS A TRIUNE BEING:
DIVINE MOTHER
DIVINE FATHER
DIVINE CHILD

They believed, however, that the essence of God, the energy or *mana* of the Creator, was comprehensible. *Mana* is a form of energy that is as real and as controllable as an electric current. It exists as a force within us and can be amplified. It also exists externally in everything in the universe and can be tapped through prayers and meditation. This force can be used to speed up the healing process and accomplish many other miraculous things.

***MANA* IS THE ESSENCE OR ENERGY OF GOD, THE CREATOR.**

There was no concept of "sin" in the ancient Hawaiʻian beliefs. One could not "sin" against God, because God was too far removed and too powerful to even bother about the sins of humans. But there was a concept of "hurt." The only "sin" to the ancient Hawaiʻian was "hurt," a hurting of oneself or another. These hurts required absolution or forgiveness. If these hurts were not cleared away, there was a danger of blocking the path between the lower physical human being and the Higher Spiritual Self.

A HUMAN BEING IS ALSO A TRIUNE BEING

The basic concept that a human being is also a triune being, as postulated by the ancient ***Huna*** teachings, is a concept that is just now being realized by modern psychologists and religionists. One way of explaining this concept in modern terms is that each human is made up of body-mind-spirit or that each human is a physical-mental-spiritual being. Another way to explain it is to say that each human has a subconscious, a conscious and a superconscious mind.

EACH HUMAN IS ALSO A TRIUNE BEING.

The discovery of the subconscious mind attributed to Sigmund Freud revolutionized the science of modern psychology. And now the superconscious mind has finally been recognized through the work of Roberto Assagioli and his Psychosynthesis, where a "connection to the transpersonal realms of soul and spirit" is valued and integrated in the work of self-discovery and healing. Many of the current "Twelve Step" programs incorporate the superconscious (Higher Self) in their strategies for personal growth and understanding. These three consciousnesses and their characteristics were known in Hawai'i centuries ago!

THE HAWAI'IANS KNEW ABOUT THE CONSCIOUS, SUBCONSCIOUS AND SUPER CONSCIOUS CENTURIES AGO!

The ancient *Kahuna* believed that life is composed of three elements: consciousness, *mana* (energy), and *aka* substance. (These are the three elements that Dr. Brigham directed Max Long to look for in his research.) When these three elements are in and around a living body, the material of the body also becomes alive. Wherever there is any form or level of consciousness, it expresses itself as life. Death comes when the consciousness-*mana-aka* was withdrawn. Death to the ancient Hawai'ian was a continuation of life in a different direction or state. It was also believed that communication between the physical world and the world of spirit was possible. The missionaries translated part of this concept as "ancestral worship," for the Hawai'ian believed they could and did communicate with their dead relatives and other spirits.

LIFE IS COMPOSED OF THREE ELEMENTS: CONSCIOUSNESS, ENERGY AND SUBSTANCE.

DEATH IS A CONTINUATION OF LIFE IN A DIFFERENT STATE.

THE KINGS WERE LINKED TO THE LAND AND THE GODS

The king was directly linked to the land and to the gods and had great *mana* or power. The chiefs and the priests were also direct links to the gods and served as transmitters of *mana* power. Other things, animate or inanimate, could also be transmitters of *mana* power. The idols of the gods, for instance, were imbued with a certain *mana*. The idols were not worshipped as the missionaries believed, but were representatives of the different aspects of Divinity and the *mana* they emanated.

Mana was often symbolized as the power of procreation. The *hula* was originally a sacred dance that honored the gods. Some historians wrote that the *hula* beguiled the gods into directing their flow of *mana* toward fruitfulness for the land and the people. The potency of the dancers depended on the power of the names and the words of the chant that accompanied the dance. It also depended on the *mana* of the person reciting the chant, the *mana* inherent in the ritual itself, the *mana* in the place where the dance and the chant were performed, and in the way the dance was delivered. The sacred *hula* dancers were originally males. The *hula* was outlawed in the 1820's because of the influence of the missionaries, who considered it lewd and evil and didn't understand the symbolism of the sacred dance. In 1999 the Roman Catholic Church voted to again allow the sacred gestures of the *hula* to be performed during designated masses.

Mana also could be used destructively. *Kahuna*, who could use their *mana* to cause pain or death, were employed as late as 1880 to 1910 to create turmoil in the political climate of the islands. Many prominent political figures of that era mysteriously died at inopportune times, usually right before elections.

THE *KAHUNA* PRAYED WITH EYES AND HANDS UPLIFTED TOWARD THE HEAVENS.

The Hawai'ian prayer, the *pule*, was not like the Christian prayer. The *Kahuna* did not petition their God as the Christian missionaries did, instead they directed the action of the prayer. They offered their prayers with the face lifted up, so the eyes could envision the gods in Heaven. The Hawai'ian extended his hands toward the sky while he projected his prayer upward. The *Kahuna pule heiau* (temple priests) taught that to bow toward the earth while praying was to look away from Heaven. It is reported that the *Kahuna* who practiced black sorcery prayed with their eyes directed downward hiding their faces from the High Self. The Christians prayed with heads bowed and hands folded, which seemed contradictory to the Hawai'ian.

THE KAHUNA UNDERSTOOD PSYCHOLOGY

The ancient *Kahuna* were not only healers, but psychologists and judges as well. They were often consulted when problems occurred in the lives of the people. They had a unique understanding of human psychology and recommended forgiveness and restitution as part of the healing process. The *Kahuna* believed that when internal beliefs are in conflict, illness follows. This concept is one that modern psychologists and other healers are just beginning to understand. Forgiveness has long been valued in most of the world's religions.

FORGIVENESS IS AN IMPORTANT PART OF THE HEALING PROCESS.

The *Kahuna* also taught that each of us has inherent psychic powers. They not only believed in these powers, which they saw not as "extra" but as basic to everyone, but they knew how and why they worked. Some *Kahuna* could psychically see into that part of the future that had already been crystallized. Others had the gift of prophecy.

They also taught that human beings had two "souls" instead of one on the earthly plane. The Christian missionaries did not understand this concept at all, for their religion centered around one "soul." Two souls made no sense to the missionaries and this concept caused great confusion in translating the *Bible*.

The oldest Hawai'ian chant, the *"Kumulipo,"* the Hawai'ian Chant of Creation, is said to have been composed upon the lost continent of *Ka Lua* (The Empire of the Sun - Mu). *"Kumulipo"* also means "origin" or "Source of Life." This chant has never been completely translated into English due to the layering of meanings in the words and phrases. The *"Kumulipo"* teaches that there were seven creative periods before the first dawn upon the earth. The Spiritual Father (*Kane*) and the Spiritual Mother (*Na Wahine*) breathed forth the cosmic eggs of Creation, from which all life on earth came into existence. (Ancient legends of other cultures speak of these same cosmic eggs.)

THE HAWAI'IAN CREATION STORY PARALLELS THE BIBLICAL CREATION STORY.

The chant tells of the creation of the species of coral and rock life that were to dwell in the Kingdom of the Sea in the First Period of Creation. The Second Period of Creation brought forth the residents of the marine kingdom and the floral life and trees on the land. The Third Period of Creation brought forth the bird life. The creeping children moved from the ocean waters to the woodlands during the Fourth Period of Creation. The Fifth, Sixth and Seventh Periods of Creation brought forth the other animals. Then in the Eighth Period of Creation *"Lai Lai,"* the first human creature, descended to earth with the first dawn. Her father was the Heavenly Father (*Kane*) and her mother the Beautiful Lady of Heaven (*Na Wahine*). From "*Lai Lai*" and the earliest humans listed in the *"Kumulipo,"* the kings and chiefs of Hawai'i trace their royal ancestry.

***LAI LAI*, A WOMAN, WAS THE FIRST HUMAN CREATURE.**

The missionaries were surprised to learn of the Hawai'ian creation story with its parallel periods of creation. They were also surprised to learn that the Hawai'ian had stories of the Biblical Flood and "Jonah and the Whale," but no stories of Jesus or the New Testament. There are several theories about these facts. Some say that the Twelve Tribes left the biblical lands before the New Testament was written. Others infer that ancient priests found their way to the islands before New Testament times, bringing with them the Old Testament stories. There are several ancient legends that tell of "white" priests arriving and staying in the islands to set up temples and schools.

From a teaching to initiates by the *Kahuna Pule Heiau* [High Priests of the Temple] comes an even older story of creation.

"At the beginning of time, long before the earth flared into existence from the sun, the space that this universe now occupies was a vortex of darkness. In the beginning there was nothing in the immensity of space but dark mists, which whirled around and around chaotically. In the cold and mist was the night world of *Po*. The only life that existed in the World of Night was the Eternal Spirit of Life, the Eternal Spirit of the Sun. The Almighty and Omnipotent *Keawe*, the Everlasting and Infinite Light of Life, and Life of the World, dwelt aloft in the Temple of the Sun at the zenith of the universe where the curving arches of the Heavens meet at its dome, in the Seventh Heaven above this earth --*Lani Uli.*

Life did not commence in the Night World of *Po* until Almighty *Keawe*, the Eternal Spirit of the Sun, breathed into it the Eternal Life of the Sun. With his first great breath of life, darkness vanished from the Upper Region of the Night World, and, in the light of the Eternal Sun, the first life dawned in the Night World of *Po*.

Keawe, being dualistic in nature, possessing all the qualities of the masculine gender and all the qualities of the feminine gender, produced a divine son, *Eli Eli*, who later became known as the god *Kane*, the Man in Heaven, or the Heavenly Father. And *Keawe* produced a Divine daughter, *Uli Uli*, who later became known as *Na Wahine*, the Beautiful Lady of Heaven, or the Heavenly Mother. Thus came into being the first Supreme and Divine Trinity of the world, who dwelt in *Kahiki Kapu I Holani Ke Ku'ina*, the Exalted Realm of *Po*."

(*Po* is described as a multi-dimensional state existing simultaneously and co-spatially with the physical realm.)

One of the most profound teachings of the ancient *Kahuna* deals with the psychology of human consciousness. In the next section we discuss the ***Huna*** teachings about the various parts of a human being and how these parts can learn to work together to become an Ideal Human Being, a fully aware, loving person in conscious contact with the Divine Source.

THE IDEAL HUMAN IS IN CONSCIOUS CONTACT WITH THE DIVINE SOURCE.

TEN PARTS OF A HUMAN

The ancient *Kahuna* believed that there are ten distinctive parts to each human being. In order to become whole, a person needed to have all ten parts working together in harmony. They were able to recognize which part was out of harmony and give advice on how to realign or heal that part.

First, there are three separate selves, minds or consciousnesses. (Modern psychology recognizes only two, the subconscious and the conscious leaving out the all-important superconscious.) Second, each self has its own special or etheric body or covering. Third, each self has its own energy. And finally, there is the physical body.

3 Selves or Consciousnesses

3 Etheric Bodies or Coverings

3 Energies or Vibrations

1 Physical Body

10 PARTS EQUAL ONE WHOLE PERSON

The three selves are called in Hawai'ian: the ***'Unihipili*** (Basic Self, Emotional Mind or Subconscious Mind); the ***'Uhane*** (Logical Self or Conscious Mind); and, the ***'Aumakua*** (the High Self or Superconscious Mind). Max Long referred to these three selves as the Low Self, the Middle Self and the High Self. In the following sections we discuss the characteristics of these three selves, their different energies and their etheric or shadowy bodies.

INNERACTIVITY

Purpose: To practice changing your perspective of awareness.

This is a guided meditation. Use whatever method you normally use to bring yourself to a meditative state before you begin. If you are working in a group, one person can read the meditation. If you are working alone, first record the meditation on an audio tape and then participate in the meditation while listening to your own voice.

Begin in a meditative state. Relax, close your eyes, and take 4 deep breaths. Picture or imagine a white sandy beach with the blue ocean waves breaking into white foam on the sand. Off in the distance you see a person standing alone. You move closer and become aware that this person is you. You see that you are wearing long denim pants and a red shirt. You see the wind whipping your hair around your head. You see the starfish you are holding in your hand.

Now shift your awareness **into** your body and look down at your bare feet. You can actually feel the wet sand squishing beneath your toes. You wiggle them and enjoy the feeling of the cool, moist sand. You feel the wind blowing your pants against your legs. You smell a faint fishy odor of seaweed that makes your nose wrinkle. Turning your head first to one side and then the other you hear the roar of the waves in your ears. It feels good to be at the beach. You take a big deep breath of the salt air.

Now move your awareness **up and out** of your body to a point about 6 feet above your head. You are now looking down on your own head. You see the top of your head, the scalp beneath your hair. You look down upon the curve of your shoulders. You can see another starfish behind you on the sand that you missed. Now move upward even higher and look far out to sea. You notice a ship in the distance and beyond that an island you didn't see before. You have a bird's eye view of the world hovering there above your lone figure on the beach. Look around in all directions and see what else you can find.

Now bring your awareness down, back down to the figure on the beach. Shift your awareness **into** your body and look down upon your toes once more and feel them wiggle. Now shift your awareness **out** of your body and move back to the point where can observe your body once more. Realize at this moment how it feels to be in a different awareness of your self. Remember these feelings.

Begin to return to the room. Take another deep breath and feel refreshed and awake. Now feel the chair around you; your feet on the floor. Take another deep breath and be fully in this moment, here, now. **Eyes open, wide awake.**

(Take a few minutes to write down anything that you want to remember about this **Inneractivity.** Which level of perception was the easiest for you to identify with? What else did you see when your awareness was far above your head? Could you shift from one awareness to another easily?)

Personal comments:

CONTINUING INNERACTIVITY

Purpose: To practice shifting your awareness.

During your own meditation practices, try shifting your awareness from one perspective to another. If you start outside your body, move into your body. If you are in your body looking out from your own inner eyes, move above your body to a point about 1-6 feet above your head. If you are above your body, expand your awareness even further to encompass the entire planet, the universe, and beyond.

Continuing Personal Comments:

O

THE PHYSICAL BODY (THE *KINO*)

The **physical body**, or ***kino*** as it is called in Hawai'ian, is the vehicle for the two consciousnesses of the *'Uhane* and the *'Unihipili* on earth. (The Hawai'ian also called these two consciousnesses "souls.") The ancient *Kahuna* believed that humans descended from the spiritual plane to the earthly plane. The purpose of life is to experience and learn and to evolve back to the spiritual plane. The material form for experience is the ***kino***. Your *'Aumakua* or High Self made the original pattern for your ***kino*** on the spiritual level. The DNA of your body is the physical programming of your Higher Self for your ***kino***. Medical science has proven that the ***kino*** renews itself constantly. Our red blood cells replenish themselves every 28 days. Our liver regenerates every six months. We have a completely new body every seven years. You are literally not the same person you were seven years ago. Your ***kino*** can also change in an instant through spontaneous healing. There are many unexplained spontaneous healings recorded in medical science and elsewhere.

WE HAVE A COMPLETELY NEW BODY EVERY SEVEN YEARS.

In her book, *Women's Bodies, Women's Wisdom,* Dr. Christiane Northrup, M.D., states that "consciousness creates the body." She states that the body is composed of dynamic energy systems, not static physical structures. Matter is the densest form of spirit and spirit is the lightest form of matter. Our bodies are manifestations of spiritual energy. Eastern practitioners have worked with the energy systems in the body for centuries.

From another Western doctor comes a modern perspective of the ***kino***. Dr. Sherwin Nuland, author of *Health from Death to Life*, is interviewed in *U.S. News & World Report*, (June 1998). He states the body is composed of 75 trillion cells with "a sophisticated coordination at a molecular level." He believes that your whole body is a unity and the purpose of that unity is to keep you alive. He states also that there is something inside us that understands the importance of unity and harmony and that we each have a biological need to create poetry. This poetry comes from our need to create harmony and rhythm, which we do using the internal organs and glands of our body. Our breath is a rhythm, our heartbeat is another. This perspective would be acceptable to the ancient *Kahuna,* for it goes beyond the apparent physical illusion of the material body towards unity and expression.

WE HAVE A BIOLOGICAL NEED TO CREATE POETRY AND RHYTHM.

The Hawaiʻian word ***"kino"*** has several meanings taken from its root words: "to emit, a bundle (of thoughts), force;" "to image;" "to concentrate thought;" "to take form, to develop;" "intensely;" and "thought." One could say that the ancient *Kahuna* believed that the ***kino*** was an "intensely energized thought form."

THE BODY IS AN "INTENSELY ENERGIZED THOUGHT FORM."

Another way to explain it is to say that the ***kino*** is your own creation and that it responds to your thoughts and emotions. You can change your health, your appearance, your moods, and your feelings by changing your thoughts. Your ***kino***, as it is today, is the outward expression of your past thoughts. Modern scientists have come to the conclusion that matter is a form of energy that can be, and is, influenced by thought, therefore, your ***kino*** is "energy influenced by thought."

From the time of birth our environment and the people around us program the ***kino*** and our two lower consciousnesses. These people stand as guides or teachers for us while we are developing our own individual judgments. There is a long-standing debate by scientists about which has the greater influence on the personality, the environment or the genes.

From the ancient Hawaiʻian we learn that each has an equally important influence. The pattern of the physical body is established prior to birth. The pattern of habits and thoughts is established from birth to about age 6. Both patterns influence the total human being for the rest of his or her life. These patterns can be changed, however. Through certain practices, negative patterns can be reprogrammed or transmuted to positive patterns, which in turn transform the ***kino***.

You can see evidence of how thoughts transform the ***kino*** by observing the faces and body language of people who are under a lot of stress. Their faces are pinched with worry and their bodies filled with tension. When they are out from under the stress, their faces soften and their bodies relax. You can also observe how the practice of meditation changes the ***kino***. Laughter and thoughts of happiness cause wonderful changes in the ***kino***.

A BODY OF LIGHT IS YOUR TRUE FORM.

As you create your physical body, your arms, legs, eyes, toes, you form an extension of your thoughts into the material world. When you add the higher aspects of spiritual thought, you begin to express and experience the Oneness of Life. Your ***kino*** changes and becomes closer to the Light Body that is your true form.

INNERACTIVITY

Purpose: To observe how thought changes the *kino*.

Take a clean piece of paper and pencil or pen and find a partner. Sit in chairs facing each other. This **Inneractivity** is done without words. Observe the face of your partner for a few minutes, making notes on a piece of paper, of how the general condition of the face especially the eyes and mouth and forehead. Your partner should keep a neutral expression on his or her face during this time.

When you are both ready, look deeply into your partner's eyes and try to make him or her laugh. You can make faces, noises (don't use any understandable words) or any kind of gesture you like. When you both have laughed, once again observe the changes in your partner's eyes, mouth, and forehead when your partner laughed and write these down. When you finish, exchange papers and share what you observed. (If you are doing this **Inneractivity** by yourself, use a mirror and observe your own face before and after.)

(Take a few minutes to write down anything that you want to remember about this **Inneractivity**. Were you able to notice any change in your partner's face? Did you notice how you felt in changing serious thoughts [observing and making notes] to silly ones [trying to make your partner laugh])?

Personal Comments:

CONTINUING INNERACTIVITY

Purpose: To practice changing your *kino*.

Since the ***kino*** is an "energized thoughtform," you can change your ***kino*** by changing your thoughts. Using the science of phrenology and related work, which study the correlation of the features of the face, head, and body in relationship to the personality, you can change any negative aspect to a positive one by using your mind to change your features.

For instance, if you find yourself more critical than you would like to be, use your mind to move your eyes wider apart. (Wide apart eyes are the features of an uncritical person.) If you would like to be more tolerant, shift the angle of the outside corner of your eye to a more upward angle. (Eyes that slant slightly upward indicate a tolerant person.) If you want to become more or less skeptical, increase or decrease the extended distance of the point of your nose in relation to the area just under your nose. (The end of the nose of skeptical people extends below the point where the nose joins the face above the lip.) Focus and imagine the features changing. Be persistent. The change may be subtle at first, but it will happen.

Continuing Personal Comments:

II

II II

THE THREE SELVES OR MINDS OR CONSCIOUSNESSES

In this discussion of the various parts of our humanness, remember that we are really talking about different parts of our whole being. By learning to integrate these parts and facilitating communication between them, endless possibilities open for us that can bring about miraculous changes in our lives. One of the purposes of life on this physical plane is to learn to integrate the body, the consciousness and the spirit into a harmonious, unified whole that recognizes the Divine working in us, through us, and as us.

The three selves are the *'**Unihipili***, the *'**Uhane*** and the ***'Aumakua***, which correspond roughly to the subconscious, the conscious and the superconscious minds. The ancient Hawai'ian believed in evolution. They believed that we progress through the various stages of life from mineral, to plant, to animal to human, and beyond. As a human, we learn first as an ***'Unihipili***, taking care of the physical body; then to an ***'Uhane***, learning how to think, guide and teach; and, then to an ***'Aumakua***, which acts as the Guardian Angel to the other selves. "Consciousness flows upward to higher and higher states emerging towards divine consciousness," states Enid Hoffman in her book, *Huna, a Beginner's Guide.* This upward flow is a good visual description of the way in which consciousness evolves.

CONSCIOUSNESS FLOWS UPWARD...

THE BASIC OR COMPANION SELF (THE 'UNIHIPILI)

The Basic Self is called the ***'Unihipili*** (Oo-nee-hee-**pee**'-lee) in Hawai'ian. It corresponds to what psychologists call the subconscious mind. A more equal term would be the Companion Self. Another good term for the ***'Unihipili*** is the "Little Sister Self" or the "Little Brother Self." The ***'Unihipili*** is the Inner Child, and what a wonderful inner child it is! It has exceptional abilities and can learn even more. It does nine-tenths of the work of the physical person. According to Max Long in his book, *Secret Science At Work*, no two ***'Unihipili*** are alike, but each one is "dear and bright and loving...endlessly faithful and willing and eager." The only way to really learn about your ***'Unihipili*** is to make a conscious effort to become acquainted with it.

> THE INNER CHILD...THE BASIC SELF...THE COMPANION SELF
> THE LITTLE SISTER OR BROTHER SELF, THE SUBCONSCIOUS
> ARE ALL NAMES FOR THE *'UNIHIPILI.*

Keep in mind when you are communicating with the ***'Unihipili*** that it is childlike and takes every word quite literally. The ***'Unihipili*** is centered in the solar plexus in the physical body. Its consciousness resides in the solar plexus, or the cell center, and uses the reticular activating system (RAS), which is a core communication system in the brain. This RAS is often referred to as the "doorkeeper to consciousness." The solar plexus acts like a broadcast and receiving station.

When Long researched the root words of ***'Unihipili,*** and the alternate word *'Uhinipili*, he found many of the characteristics of the subconscious self, as modern psychology understands it, and additional characteristics as the ancient *Kahuna* understood it.

- ❖ 1. It is a separate and conscious spirit.
- ❖ 2. It is a spirit that is connected to arms and legs.
- ❖ 3. It generates the emotions.
- ❖ 4. It is able to grieve.
- ❖ 5. It cannot talk.
- ❖ 6. It is something that covers up something else and hides it or is hidden by a cover or a veil.
- ❖ 7. It is a spirit that accompanies another and is joined to it.
- ❖ 8. It is sticky or adheres to something.
- ❖ 9. It can attach itself to another and acts as its servant.
- ❖ 10. It does things secretly, silently and very carefully.
- ❖ 11. It does not do certain things because it is afraid of offending the gods.
- ❖ 12. It can protrude from something, can rise up from that something and can draw something out of something, like a coin
- ❖ 13. It desires certain things most earnestly.

❖ 14. It is stubborn and unwilling.

❖ 15. It is disposed to refuse to do as it is told.

❖ 16. It tinctures or impregnates or mixes completely with something else.

❖ 17. It is connected with the slow dripping of water and with the manufacture and exudation of nourishing water (milk of the mother).

❖ 18. It can remember everything.

❖ 19. It has only elementary reasoning power.

❖ 20. It accepts and reacts to hypnotic suggestion.

❖ 21. It has a low voltage of vital force (*mana*).

1. **It is a separate and conscious spirit.** As you become better acquainted with your ***'Unihipili***, you will realize that it is indeed a different part of you and can act quite independently from your logical mind. You may have experienced times when you talked to yourself and received answers. You were communicating with your ***'Unihipili*** without realizing it.

2. **It is connected to arms and legs.** The ***'Unihipili*** is completely enmeshed in the physical body and controls all the various processes of the physical body, except the voluntary muscles. In fact, its center of consciousness is in the body, more precisely the solar plexus. Whenever you are feeling sensation in your solar plexus, you will know that your awareness is with the ***'Unihipili***. The ***'Unihipili*** is fully in charge of the physical body. It never sleeps, it is always on duty making sure the body is functioning. It has been described as being in the body as a pencil is in its case.

3. **It generates the emotions.** The ***'Unihipili*** is the self that cries. Every time you are feeling emotion, you are in the awareness of the ***'Unihipili***. It is the seat of the emotions. Love, hate, fear, anger, and joy all come from the ***'Unihipili.*** Sometimes they are so strong that they sweep away the Will of the Conscious Mind, the *'Uhane*, and force it into joining with the strong emotions. You no doubt have seen someone who is in the throes of such strong emotions that no amount of logic can reach them. Children are often in this state because their *'Uhane* has not yet developed enough strength to control their ***'Unihipili***.

4. **It is able to grieve.** Sadness is a highly charged emotion. Grieving comes naturally to the ***'Unihipili*** as it tends to dwell on the sad things in life, unless encouraged and uplifted by the thoughts of the *'Uhane*. Tears flow easily from the deep feelings of the ***'Unihipili*** and it grieves, not only for itself, but also for others.

5. **It is not able to talk.** The ***'Unihipili*** does not control speech. It does however control music and singing, which is more precisely rhythm and patterns. It communicates instead with

pictures or images and emotions. These pictures or images are the ones sent or received during telepathic communication. The *'**Unihipili*** is the telepathic communicator.

6. It is something that covers up something else and hides it or is hidden by a cover or a veil. The something that is covered up is the *'Uhane*, the conscious self. The cover or veil is the physical body, the *kino*.

7. It is a spirit that accompanies another and is joined to it. The *'**Unihipili*** accompanies the *'Uhane* throughout life. It is joined together with the *'Uhane* and cleaves to it as if the two parts were glued together.

8. It is sticky or adheres to something. This is a description of the ability of the *'**Unihipili*** to reach out with its shadowy body or *aka* body as a finger reaches out to touch something. This *aka* substance is sticky. (We will discuss the *aka* bodies in another section.)

9. It can attach itself to another and acts as its servant. The *'**Unihipili*** is attached to the *'Uhane* within the physical body and acts as the servant for the *'Uhane*. The *'**Unihipili*** has certain abilities that the *'Uhane* does not have, such as the ability to control the *kino* and do other things as directed by the *'Uhane*.

10. It does things secretly, silently and very carefully. One of the characteristics of the *'**Unihipili*** is that it works in silence. It cannot speak. Sometimes it does things that it secretly hides from the *'Uhane*, such as not following an order because it feels guilt about the subject. It is a careful and meticulous librarian, which stores all the memories in its *aka* body.

11. It does not do certain things because it is afraid of offending the gods. The *'**Unihipili*** is the storehouse for guilt. If it is feeling guilty about something, it hides its face in shame from "God." Much of the guilt the *'**Unihipili*** feels is caused during early childhood before the *'Uhane* became strong. Unthinking adults caused it to feel guilty and shamed the childlike part for certain behaviors. These guilts become complexes or fixations that are hidden from the conscious mind and still affect us as adults.

12. It can protrude from something, can rise up from that something, and can draw something out of something, like a coin from a pocket. This refers to the psychic ability of the *'**Unihipili***. There is a natural inherent psychic ability in all of us. The *'**Unihipili*** has control of this ability. It can reach out and learn things using senses that are beyond the traditional five senses of the physical body. (How the *'**Unihipili*** does this will be discussed in the section on *aka* bodies.)

13. It desires things most earnestly. The *'**Unihipili*** has all the emotions. Desire is an emotion. Whenever we want something, an earnest desire comes into play in order for us to receive what we want. We must communicate with our *'**Unihipili*** in order to get its emotional cooperation for our goal. Emotions generate energy and energy is necessary in the process of creation.

14. It is stubborn and unwilling. Many times what we want with our head is not what we want with our heart. When this happens, our *'**Unihipili*** will not cooperate. It becomes quite stubborn and unwilling to do what it is asked. This is one of the most important reasons to develop honest communication and compassionate understanding between the Selves.

15. It is disposed to refuse to do as it is told. The ***ʻUnihipili*** often acts like a stubborn child, refusing to do what it is told. Sometimes it pouts. It would much rather be asked to help rather than be told to help. This is another important area for good communication. Getting the cooperation of our ***ʻUnihipili*** in advance avoids problems later.

16. It tinctures or impregnates or mixes completely with something else. The consciousness of the ***ʻUnihipili*** interfaces with every cell and tissue of the physical body or *kino*, including the brain. It also mixes completely with the *ʻUhane* in the *kino*.

17. It is connected with the slow dripping of water and with the manufacture and exudation of nourishing water (milk of the mother). The *Kahuna* used water as the symbol for vital force or energy. This water or "milk of the mother" comes from the ***ʻUnihipili,*** which manufactures the energy from the food we eat and the air we breathe. It is like mother's milk to us as it sustains and nourishes us in the physical realm. The ***ʻUnihipili*** is in charge of the body fluids and drips water when it cries.

18. It can remember everything. Scientists have determined that the subconscious records everything it hears, sees, smells, tastes, touches, and feels from before birth. In fact, it is recording all the time whether we are awake or asleep and even when we are under anesthesia. It is an excellent bio-computer. The ***ʻUnihipili*** records all this information as patterns and stores it in tiny bits of its *aka* body to be recalled at the appropriate, and sometimes inappropriate, moment. These bits of *aka* are stored with other similar bits of information much like a cluster of grapes. The *Kahuna* used a cluster of grapes or berries as the symbol for memories. This explains how memories are linked to each other around a common theme. You could say that the ***ʻUnihipili*** exists in the past as it remembers everything that it has ever recorded.

19. It has only elementary reasoning power. The ***ʻUnihipili*** uses deductive reasoning. The ***ʻUnihipili*** reasons as a child. Many times this method of reasoning produces incorrect conclusions, especially if it is based on misinformation learned earlier in life or based solely on emotional reactions.

20. It accepts and reacts to hypnotic suggestion. The ***ʻUnihipili*** (the subconscious mind) is the part of us that accepts hypnotic suggestions. Actually, it accepts all suggestions. We use the suggestibility of the ***ʻUnihipili*** when we use affirmations to improve our reactions to ideas and feelings or strive to reach certain goals. The ***ʻUnihipili*** also reacts to mesmeric suggestions. When a person is hypnotized, the *ʻUhane* is bypassed and the suggestion goes straight to the ***ʻUnihipili.***

21. It has a low voltage of vital force. The ***ʻUnihipili*** manufactures and uses the lowest voltage of vital force, or *mana* as it is called in Hawaiʻian. This *mana* can be transferred to objects or to other people. It can also be used to charge ideas, suggestions and prayers. It is the same vital force that is used by healers. This energy can be used to invigorate others who may be low in energy or aid in the healing process.

It is extremely important for us to become familiar with all the characteristics of the ***'Unihipili***, so that we will know how to best communicate with it and enlist its cooperation. The ***'Unihipili*** is your childlike part, skilled in taking care of the physical body, eager to please you, but often hindered by guilt not of its own making. It is enmeshed in the physical body or *kino*, but can extend a part of itself outward to touch other objects or people. It is the Little Sister or Little Brother who needs guidance. It generates, stores, distributes, and transmits energy or *mana*. It is the psychic part of you. It contains all the memories. It generates all your emotions. It is indeed a wonderful and talented part of you that deserves honor and respect!

YOUR *'UNIHIPILI* IS YOUR EMOTIONAL SELF.

The most important aspect of the *'Unihipili* is the fact that it, <u>and it alone</u>, has the ability to contact the *'Aumakua*, your Higher Self. In other words, any prayers you send to God, can only be sent by the *'Unihipili*. It is vital to your well being and critical to your spiritual growth that you learn to communicate with your *'Unihipili*.

INNERACTIVITY

Purpose: To become familiar with how the *'Unihipili* generates emotion.

First, ask your ***'Unihipili*** if it would like to play a game with you. We will assume it has answered "yes." Explain to your ***'Unihipili*** that for the next five minutes you, the ***'Uhane***, will name the emotion and your ***'Unihipili*** will generate the feeling of that emotion. The object is to see how many different emotions you can name and generate. The winner gets a prize. (You decide on the prize, something that your *'Unihipili* will like.)

(Take a few minutes to write down anything that you want to remember about this **Inneractivity**. How many different emotions did you experience? Was it difficult for you to feel any emotion? What other thoughts, ideas, memories or emotions came to you during this time? Was it easy for you to engage your ***'Unihipili*** in this game?)

Personal Comments:

THE MIDDLE SELF OR LOGICAL SELF (THE '*UHANE*)

The ***'Uhane*** (Oo-**hah**'-nay) is the thinking part of you that speaks. According to James Venable Alexander, a Certified ***Huna*** Practitioner and Teacher, .a good way to think about your ***'Uhane*** is to remember that "your ***'Uhane*** is in your mouth." It is able to vocalize its thoughts. It is described as the logical part of you. It has no emotions, only thoughts. Its center is in the brain, actually in the "new brain" or forebrain, residing in the left hemisphere. The language skills come from the left hemisphere of the brain. The ***'Uhane*** is logical, analytical and work oriented. Being a guest in the *kino*, it <u>cannot and does not</u> control any of the physical body processes. It is older than the *'Unihipili* and wiser. It is the Older Sister or Older Brother who offers guidance to the Little Sister or Little Brother. It is the teacher of the *'Unihipili.*

THE *'UHANE* IS YOUR OLDER BROTHER OR SISTER.

According to Max Long, the duty of the ***'Uhane*** is "to make plans for the task of living and see that proper effort is made to achieve" such plans. When a person is born, the ***'Uhane*** is very weak. It takes time to grow strong. We call this the maturing process. The ***'Uhane*** develops its full strength at about age twelve, (Plato's "age of reason"). Up to that point the *'Unihipili* controls the human being. You see evidence of this in children, and some adults, who let their emotions rule. The ***'Uhane*** must grow and become strong in order to manage the powerful emotions that often get the *'Unihipili* into trouble.

In Long's research of the root words that make up the word ***'Uhane,*** he found the following characteristics:

- 1. It is a separate and conscious spirit.
- 2. It is a spirit, which can talk, even when not connected to the body.
- 3. It has the ability to use the power of words.
- 4. It is a pipe or channel for water.
- 5. It is able to grieve.
- 6. It cannot remember a thought after it leaves its center of attention.
- 7. It uses inductive reasoning.
- 8. It cannot be hypnotized.
- 9. It has the power to use Will of the hypnotic kind.
- 10. It is a guide or teacher.
- 11. It has a certain vital force of a medium voltage (*mana-mana*).

1. **It is a separate and conscious spirit.** When you think of your "self," you usually think of that part of you located in your mind. This is often referred to as the "ego." It is our normal identity. Some psychologists believe that this is the superior part of the human being. The *Kahuna* believed that it was superior only in the sense that it was older and wiser.

2. **It is a spirit, which can talk, even when not connected to the body.** This is the part of you that speaks and has the ability to form and vocalize words. When the spirit has left the physical body, the ***'Uhane*** can still speak.

3. **It has the ability to use the power of words.** Words contain energy. When they are spoken, they release that energy. Certain words used by many people over the centuries are extremely powerful, such as specific prayers or phrases. When you hear certain poems, political speeches or religious readings, you may feel emotional. The power contained in words is especially important in making a prayer.

4. **It is a pipe or channel for water.** This refers to being a channel for energy. Water was the symbol for energy or vital force. Water was used by many ancient cultures as a symbol for this force. The energy of the ***'Uhane*** is called *mana-mana* in Hawai'ian, the doubling of the word indicating it is more powerful.

5. **It is able to grieve.** The ***'Uhane*** grieves, but not with the emotions of the *'Unihipili*. For example, it can join in the emotion of sadness as an understanding of regret. The ***'Uhane*** does not shed tears.

6. **It cannot remember a thought after it leaves its center of attention.** The ***'Uhane***, it could be said, exists in the present at all times. It is only aware of what is happening now in its center of attention. Once a thought has left this center, the ***'Uhane*** must rely on the *'Unihipili* to get it back as a memory. When the thought or memory returns, the ***'Uhane*** is aware that it is a past memory. Often the ***'Uhane*** requests a specific memory but the memory is stored in the "library archives" and it takes time for the *'Unihipili* to find it. This explains why you sometimes can't remember something until a few hours later and it suddenly enters your mind. The ***'Uhane***, although it cannot remember, has the ability to use memories to create or imagine.

7. **It uses inductive reasoning.** This reasoning is far superior to the reasoning of the *'Unihipili*, for this reasoning moves from the specific to the general. It uses logic to arrive at its conclusions. It is this inductive reasoning capability that sets human beings apart from the animal kingdom.

8. **It cannot be hypnotized.** The ***'Uhane*** cannot be hypnotized. It can, however, be put to sleep. In fact, it is the ***'Uhane*** that goes to sleep every night. The *'Unihipili* never sleeps. It is also the part of us that is influenced the most by alcohol and drugs. Losing one's inhibitions under the influence of alcohol or drugs indicates that the ***'Uhane*** has lost the power of control over the *'Unihipili's* actions and one feels more "free" and "loose." Addictions represent the ***'Uhane's*** almost total loss of control over the *'Unihipili.*

9. **It has the power to use Will of the hypnotic kind.** Will is the most important characteristic of the ***'Uhane***. It is this Will that controls the *'Unihipili* and directs the

energy. Will is also the force that directs suggestions, either mild or hypnotic. Leading psychologists have placed the Will at the center of personal growth and development.

10. It is a guide or teacher. The ***'Uhane*** stands as a teacher in relation to the *'Unihipili*. The ***'Uhane*** teaches the *'Unihipili* the things it must know in order to evolve. The ***'Uhane*** is in control of the expression of the feelings. For the first 10-12 years of the life of the *kino* the *'Unihipili* is in control. As the ***'Uhane*** grows in understanding and strength it begins to take over control and is more able to direct the *'Unihipili* in the proper way of living. It is the major job of the ***'Uhane*** to learn to control the *'Unihipili* and not let it run away with the person. But it must do this with love and understanding, not coercion and force.

11. It has a certain vital force of the medium voltage. This is *mana-mana*, more powerful than the *mana* of the *'Unihipili*. Scientists have recorded the electrical currents in the body and found a low voltage in the body tissues and a higher voltage in the brain. This higher voltage in the brain is the *mana-mana*. It is not yet known how the ***'Uhane*** steps up this energy to a higher voltage. It is used for creating thought and is the force behind the Will.

THE *'UHANE* IS YOUR THINKING AND SPEAKING SELF.

The ***'Uhane*** is the logical and reasoning part of a person. The ***'Uhane's*** role is to be guide and teacher to the *'Unihipili*. It uses imagination and Will to help create the new patterns or molds that produce change. It is the responsibility of the ***'Uhane*** to insure the growth and evolvement of the *'Unihipili,* as well as its own. This is an ongoing process and is achieved in many ways. The first and most important way is to learn to communicate with the *'Unihipili* and begin to develop the trust necessary to become a team. The two Selves together are stronger and more powerful than the one separate from the other.

THE TWO SELVES TOGETHER ARE STRONGER AND MORE POWERFUL!

INNERACTIVITY

Purpose: To begin a dialogue between the *'Uhane* and the *'Unihipili.*

Take out a clean sheet of paper and a pencil or pen. On the front side of the paper write in cursive a short letter from your ***'Uhane*** to your ***'Unihipili.*** Say anything you want, but make it personal. A good way to start is to let your ***'Unihipili*** know that you are interested in working with it and learning how to communicate better. Express some thoughts of love and reassurance. Read the letter out loud to your ***'Unihipili*** when you have completed it.

On the reverse side of the paper write a short letter back from your ***'Unihipili*** to your ***'Uhane*** answering the first letter. This time use your other hand and print the answer. Let the feelings of the ***'Unihipili*** come out onto the paper without making judgments. Listen carefully and write down the first inner responses you receive from your ***'Unihipili.*** Thank your *'Unihipili* for doing this inneractivity with you.

(Take a few minutes to write down anything that you want to remember about this **Inneractivity**. Did your ***'Unihipili*** cooperate with your ***'Uhane***? Did you feel any emotion when the first letter was read aloud? Did you get a sense of a different part within you?)

Personal Comments:

CONTINUING INNERACTIVITY

Purpose: To explore the inner dialogue between your *'Unihipili* and your *'Uhane*.

Keep a diary for the next 6 months and write short notes from your *'Uhane* to your *'Unihipili*, and the answers back. Write notes about any situations that may come up where you are not exactly sure how your *'Unihipili* feels about the circumstances or people involved. After 30 days, plan a quiet time and re-read the entries you made. Observe how you have become more aware of the feelings of your *'Unihipili* about certain situations and if he or she is becoming more comfortable in communicating feelings with you. Be sure to thank your *'Unihipili* for its cooperation each time you write the notes.

Continuing Personal Comments:

THE HIGHER SELF OR GUARDIAN ANGEL (THE 'AUMAKUA)

According to Dr. Otha Wingo, Director of Huna Research, Inc., "we know we have a connection with the Divine. We don't always know it is a part of us." The ***'Aumakua*** (Ah-oo-mah-**koo'**-ah) is that realization of the Divine within us. It is that part of us that is our Higher Self. It is our connection with the spiritual realm. It is the third part of the trinity of humankind. Some teachings refer to the Higher Self as the "Soul." It is, in psychological terms, our superconscious mind. The ***'Aumakua*** is centered in the right hemisphere of the brain. This part of the brain governs the unconscious processes, spatial perception, understanding of whole systems, and is the center for intuition, inspiration and creativity. According to Enid Hoffman in her book, *Huna, a Beginner's Guide*, she states that "the High Self is able to see your life as a whole and the interrelationships of all the events within it." She explains further that your ***'Aumakua*** has access to all the information you need to become "self-actualized" and "self-realized."

THE *'AUMAKUA* IS THE REALIZATION OF THE DIVINE WITHIN US.

The *Kahuna* taught the basic truth that the Divine Essence is in everything and that everything is a part of the Divine. They also taught that "the human mind is not capable of understanding a form of consciousness unlike and superior to its own...," so there is no way we can possibly comprehend Ultimate God. As we ascend to higher planes of consciousness, we are able to comprehend more of the Divine.

We do have the ability, however, with our present consciousness, to conceive of and be aware of, the next level of Divinity above us. This is the level of the ***'Aumakua***. The ***'Aumakua*** stands as the symbol of God for us. It is a godlike spirit that desires to help us in every way possible. The ***'Aumakua*** could be defined as your personal God. All prayers, no matter to whom they are sent, go first to your own Higher Self, your ***'Aumakua***. If your ***'Aumakua*** cannot answer your prayer, it will seek the aid of the greater company of ***'Aumakua (the Po'e 'Aumakua)*** or the Higher Beings.

One Hawai'ian definition of ***'Aumakua*** is "a living person's deceased ancestor, who has become a god." The ***'Aumakua*** is that part of you, on the continuum, which has graduated into the spiritual plane. In ancient Hawai'i, and even today, each family clan, or *'ohana,* has a special ***'Aumakua***, represented by an animal or element of nature. This ***'Aumakua*** is believed to protect and care for the family and is also prayed to for assistance.

Long defines the ***'Aumakua*** as the "Utterly Trustworthy Parental Spirit." The ***'Aumakua*** is a parent spirit and contains both negative and positive polarities, both Mother and Father (Male and Female). It is utterly trustworthy and stands ready to help the two Selves in its care at all times. It is a "unifying and integrating influence." According to Long, the ***'Aumakua*** is not worshipped - it is **LOVED!**

Another term for describing the ***'Aumakua*** is "Guardian Angel." According to a recent issue of *Time Magazine*, 69% of all Americans believe in angels and 49% know they have a personal Guardian Angel. This personal Guardian Angel watches over us, protects us and helps us all through life. This is a partial description of the ***'Aumakua*** and the personal God that the Hawai'ians knew.

The ancient *Kahuna* also taught that there is an ***'Aumakua*** for different groups, such as an ***'Aumakua*** for sharks, an ***'Aumakua*** for clouds, an ***'Aumakua*** for fire, plants, volcanoes, rivers, families, countries, etc. Some other esoteric teachings call these "Group Souls." Prayers could be sent to these special ***'Aumakua*** to enlist their aid. There are many authenticated reports of lava being diverted through prayer, sharks and turtles called in to shore, weather changing for the better, drowned people brought back to life, and even more miraculous happenings attributed to these ***'Aumakua***.

The ***'Aumakua*** is our link with the spiritual plane where energy or *mana* is abundant. High *mana* or *mana-loa* continuously flows over, around and through us from our ***'Aumakua***. In some inexplicable way this energy sustains and nourishes us while we are alive to this physical existence.

Long researched the following characteristics of the ***'Aumakua*** using the root words and also the terms *Akua-noho* ("the god who dwells with men") and *Akua-ulu* ("the god who inspires men"):

♦ 1. It is a separate and conscious spirit.

♦ 2. It is a higher spirit or being.

♦ 3. It is the older, entirely trustworthy parental self.

♦ 4. It is attached to the body, but not in it.

♦5. It is the spirit that answers all prayers.

♦ 6. It is a high point of land, a period of time, a condition in which one is entirely engaged in a certain course of action or course of conduct.

♦ 7. It entwines as a vine.

♦ 8. It has the power of realization.

♦ 9. It knows the past, the present, and the future that has already been crystallized.

♦ 10. It can change the future.

♦ 11. It is the source of all healing.

♦ 12. It has a high voltage of vital force or mana (*mana-loa*).

1. **It is a separate and conscious spirit.** The word "separate" is used only to distinguish the characteristics of the three spirits that make up the complete human being. The ***'Aumakua*** is distinctly different from the other two consciousnesses but is closely connected to them.

2. **It is a higher spirit or being.** The ***'Aumakua*** exists on the next level of consciousness. It has evolved upward from the *'Uhane* consciousness. It exists in the spiritual realm but is connected to the physical realm.

3. **It is the older, entirely trustworthy parental spirit.** It is the concept of *Father-Mother-God* often used by other religions. This older spirit stands as guide and teacher to the *'Uhane* as the *'Uhane* stands as guide and teacher to the *'Unihipili*. It has a body of light and is made up of both male and female energies. When we graduate as a *'Uhane* to become an ***'Aumakua***, we are reunited with that complimentary part of us (either male or female) to become a single entity containing both aspects. This is similar to the soul mate idea of other esoteric teachings.

4. **It is attached to the body, but not in it.** The ***'Aumakua*** does not reside in the *kino*, but stays close to it. It maintains contact with the physical body through a cord of *aka* substance, often seen as the Silver Cord. The body of the ***'Aumakua*** is a body of light and is sometimes seen as a glowing ball of energy.

5. **It is the spirit that answers prayers.** All prayers go first to the ***'Aumakua*** no matter to whom they are addressed. The ***'Aumakua*** has the ability to bring answers to prayers into material or physical form. A prayer is an important ritual and a vital part of the life of a human being. (We discuss the ***Huna*** Prayer in another section).

6. **It is a high point of land, a period of time, an action of mind, a condition in which one is entirely engaged in a certain course of action or course of conduct.** The symbols of a high point of land (a mountain), and a period of time are symbols of the Higher Self. The ***'Aumakua*** is the "fully formed idea in action." The meanings of the root words have to do with transformation and completed action. The ***'Aumakua*** is always in a state of readiness to assist the *'Unihipili* and *'Uhane*. You could say that the ***'Aumakua*** lives in the future because it brings into fruition a fully formed future idea.

7. **It entwines as a vine**. The ***'Aumakua*** entwines itself with the other two Selves, nourishing them as a vine nourishes its fruit. The vine is also a symbol of *mana* or energy.

8. **It has the power of realization.** The mentation of the ***'Aumakua*** is beyond our comprehension. The closest we can come to understanding it is to the use the word "realization." To realize is to make actual. The ***'Aumakua*** has the power to bring about desires into form. However, the ***'Aumakua*** will not interfere with the desires of the other two Selves unless it is asked. In other words, each person has free will.

9. **It knows the past, the present, and the future that has already been crystallize.** The ***'Aumakua*** is not bound by time and space. It is not bound by the other "laws" of the physical world. It can see time in any direction, including into that part of the future that has already begun to take form.

10. **It can change the future.** It is a well-known fact that we create our own reality. Creating on the spiritual level and bringing that reality into physical form is the great ability of the ***'Aumakua.*** The ***'Aumakua*** is ready to change the future for the other two Selves, but it has to know what future they desire. In other words, the ***'Aumakua*** must know the pattern before it can begin its work to build the future circumstances.

11. **It is the source of all healing.** The ***'Aumakua*** has the ability to change the physical. It is that powerful! When you think about it, a prayer for healing is a request for a change in a future condition - to a condition of health.

12. **It has a high voltage of vital force or *mana*.** This high voltage of vital force, or *mana-loa*, is of the atom-splitting kind. The ***'Aumakua*** has power of which we cannot even conceive and uses this power or energy to heal, change circumstances, and create anything you desire. Scientists have not yet measured this *mana loa,* however, they continue to search for the "power" of creation.

BECOME THE COMPLETE TRIUNE BEING YOU ARE MEANT TO BE.

The superconscious or ***'Aumakua*** is the missing link in modern science. It is the spiritual part of the human with the great ability to create. It is that part of us that is connected to God. It resides outside the physical body, but is always near to us. It is our Guardian Angel, forever trustworthy, always available to us for guidance and teaching, always available for aid and assistance. It answers all prayers and calls on other Higher Beings for help when needed. It exists outside of space and time. It can see into the future and share that with us through premonitions, intuitions, and signs. It can change our future, but must wait until it is requested to do so by the other two Selves. It is the source of all healing. When you learn to contact your ***'Aumakua*** and invite the spiritual to become a part of your life, your life will be changed forever. You are on your way to becoming the complete and whole triune being you are meant to be.

INNERACTIVITY

Purpose: To make contact with your *'Aumakua*.

This is a guided meditation that leads you through the steps necessary to contact your

'Aumakua. (If you are doing this exercise at home, record the meditation first or have a friend read it as you participate in this **Inneractivity**.)

Center yourself and enter a meditative state. Ask your *'Unihipili* to join you in this **Inneractivity** and assist you to experience the presence of your ***'Aumakua.***

As you continue to breathe in and breathe out slowly and deeply, you realize you are standing in a beautiful garden, a secret garden you have never been in before. You look down and see a garden path that takes you among the flowers and trees. The flowers are all in bloom and you can smell their heavenly fragrances in the air as you pass by. Tall trees overhead are casting soft shadows on the stones of the path as you walk along. You pause to admire first one flower and then another. The flowers are so delicate and beautiful here in this garden. You just stand for a moment breathing in the peace and beauty of this -- your Secret Garden. You look around and ahead of you on the path you see an ancient stone temple. It seems like it has been standing in this garden for a long, long time waiting for you to find it. You approach the temple and put your hand on the cool stones of the wall and feel the strength in the carved rocks. You notice a door to your right that is hidden behind some trailing vines. You push the vines away and stand a moment wondering if you should go in or not. Something inside of you urges you to go on, to open the door and see what is hidden there. You push against it and it slowly creaks open to reveal a bare, inner room.

In the center of the room is a small stone altar. On the altar is a glowing lamp. The flame is very low, but burns with a beautiful light. You walk over to the altar and a miraculous thing begins to happen. The closer you move towards the altar the brighter and higher the flame burns. You suddenly realize that this is the flame of your Higher Self, the essence of that part of you that radiates Divine Love, that has been burning here undiscovered by you until now. You stand near the altar and stretch your arms upward toward the Heavens and deeply breath in warmth of the flame of your Higher Self. As you breathe in the light, you breathe in the knowledge that you can never be separated again from your true essence, your Divine essence. And with that knowledge you become aware that the flame has now transformed into a Being of pure Light, radiating a love you have felt before but never with this much intensity. You let the radiance of this pure love pour into you and the pure love within your own heart begins to respond. You feel that your heart is overflowing with the precious love for your ***'Aumakua***, your Higher Self. Your body and your mind and your heart become one with the Love of this Radiant Light. In this timeless moment you remember who and what you really are and you give thanks for that remembering.

Slowly, slowly the Light withdraws and you are back in the temple looking at the flame burning upon the altar. You know the feeling of love and harmony you have experienced here will stay with you for the rest of your days. You know that anytime you want to experience this feeling of Love you have but to walk down the garden path and enter the Temple of Light. You bow in reverence and turn towards the door. You step back through the door and find you are holding the hand of your dear Little Sister or Little Brother. You smile at each other and feel the same pure love growing between you. You walk down the garden path together to return to this moment. You now know that in order to find the Temple of Light you must enter the garden together and you are grateful for the help of your Companion Self. At the garden gate you stop and give your Little Sister or Little Brother a heartfelt hug and take your separate paths back to the present.

Take a deep breath and begin to return to this room. Feel refreshed in body, mind and spirit. Feel the love that you shared with your Companion Self and your Higher Self. Feel the chair solid beneath your body. Start to move your fingers and toes and awaken to be here and now. **Eyes open,**

wide awake.

(Take a few minutes to write down anything you want to remember about this **Inneractivity**. Will you be able to find the garden and the Temple of Light again? How did the pure love of your ***'Aumakua*** make you feel? Did you know beforehand that you needed your *'Unihipili* to go with you?)

Personal Comments:

CONTINUING INNERACTIVITY

Purpose: To invite the *'Aumakua* to take its rightful place in your life.

In order for the ***'Aumakua*** to take its place in the human trinity, it must be invited or asked. In its role as a Guardian Angel, the ***'Aumakua*** is always close at hand ready to uplift and guide and protect the other Selves. To invite the presence of your ***'Aumakua*** into your life is to become aware that there is more to you than just the physical and mental. You acknowledge and accept the Divinity within you. All you have to do is ask, and it shall be granted. This **Continuing Inneractivity** is to make two daily prayers inviting the ***'Aumakua*** into your life. Recite one in the morning before you start your day, and recite the other in the evening just before you go to sleep. These prayerful invitations should include your *'Unihipili*, by referring to yourself as "we" in the recitation. The two of you can return to the Temple of Light in your secret garden or go to another centering place you both agree upon. In this sacred place, make your prayer and invite your ***'Aumakua*** to become a part of your life. Visualize whatever symbol you wish to use to represent the presence of the ***'Aumakua*** in your life.

Write your prayer of invitation here:

Write your picture or image here:

Continuing Personal Comments:

THE THREE SHADOWY BODIES (THE *AKA* BODIES)

Aka means "shadow" in Hawaiʻian and the *Kahuna* used this word to describe the substance out of which the etheric doubles or the auric bodies of the subconscious and conscious are made. Actually, everything has an ***aka*** body, including thoughts.

EVERYTHING HAS AN *AKA* BODY, EVEN THOUGHTS.

Aka also means "a luminous extension away from the body;" or "a halo of light around the moon or sun;" or "a circle of light extending from the moon or sun before it rises above the horizon." It also means "transparent," "reflection," "mirror" or "essence."

Recently, scientists mathematically confirmed a theory, called "the strings theory," that states everything in the universe is connected by "strings." The ancient *Kahuna* knew of these "strings," which they called ***aka*** threads, centuries ago. The ***aka*** substance has the characteristic of being sticky and stringy. It can attach itself to other objects or people like chewing gum that can be stretched out. It can also be pulled very thin, much like a strand of spider silk. It is the spider that symbolizes this ***aka*** substance in ancient Egyptian hieroglyphics. Spider Woman is an important Native American deity. It is this ***aka*** substance of which the Silver Cord is made. (The Silver Cord is the name for the connecting cord between the *ʻUnihipili* and the *ʻAumakua*).

Aka has certain qualities. It can attach and stick to something. It can be pulled out like threads. ***Aka*** threads carry chemical substances from one person to another. They are also used to send and receive telepathic messages and impressions. ***Aka*** acts as the container for *mana* or energy. ***Aka*** cords or threads are great conductors of *mana*.

AKA CORDS CONDUCT MANA.

Does this mean that prayers sent to the *'Aumakua* along the ***aka*** cord are telepathic? Yes, indeed! In fact, **all prayers are telepathic!** This may seem like a strange idea, but when you pray you project your thoughts and your desires towards the Divine. This is communication between consciousnesses and you don't use any of the five physical senses to accomplish it. It can best be described as telepathic.

The three Selves remain in their ***aka*** bodies after the death of the *kino*. Together they either reincarnate or move onward to graduate. Graduation means to move into the next level of consciousness. The *'Unihipili* is promoted to a *'Uhane*, the *'Uhane* is promoted to an *'Aumakua* and the *'Aumakua* graduates to a higher level of consciousness. A new *'Unihipili* emerges from the animal kingdom to take its beginning position in the human trinity and in the continuum of your life stream.

The *AKA* BODY OF THE *'UNIHIPILI*

The ***aka*** body of the *'Unihipili* is the most versatile. It is denser than that of the *'Uhane*. It interpenetrates the physical body, molecule for molecule and cell for cell, making an exact replica or pattern of the *kino*. All healing is accomplished through this pattern. It extends about 1/2 inch outside the *kino* and is seen by some aura readers. The ***aka*** body of the *'Unihipili* exists in the same space as the *kino*. ***Aka*** is a conductor of low vital force energy or *mana*.

ALL HEALING IS ACCOMPLISHED THROUGH THE PATTERN OF THE *AKA* BODY OF THE *'UNIHIPILI*.

The *'Unihipili* can extend a finger of its ***aka*** substance and locate and "read" information about an object or a person. This extension is also accomplished by looking through the eyes, hearing a sound, smelling, or feeling something.

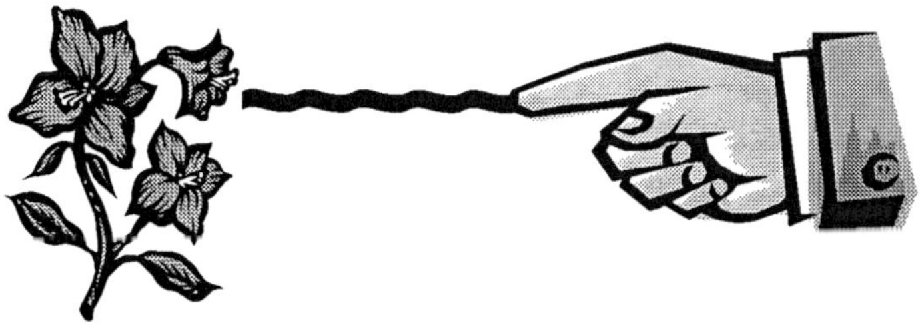

Aka also extends by thinking about a person or an object. The full awareness of the five physical senses can be projected with this ***aka*** finger or the entire ***aka*** body can be disconnected from the physical body, during astral travel, except for an anchoring cord of ***aka*** substance.

Analyzing and measuring another person's character, personality or intelligence is another ability the *'Unihipili* uses via the ***aka*** threads. It also measures relationships to surrounding objects, texture, temperature, etc. It is the *'Unihipili* in its ***aka*** body that makes dowsing and remote viewing possible. It is the substance used for all psychic abilities.

The *'Unihipili* sends and receives telepathic messages along the ***aka*** threads. Every time we touch or think about an object or a person we attach an ***aka*** thread. The more contact we have with an object or person the more ***aka*** threads we attach. These eventually become braided into ***aka*** cords. As the ***aka*** threads strengthen, they become excellent conductors of vital force or *mana*.

The *'Unihipili* uses ***aka*** to store bits of information and memories in its body/cell-library. Memories and complexes are carried over into the spirit life after death in the ***aka*** body of the *'Unihipili*. Therefore, it is important to rid the *'Unihipili* of the guilt complexes before death.

THE *AKA* BODY OF THE *'UHANE*

The ***aka*** body of the *'Uhane* is lighter or less dense than that of the *'Unihipili.* It interpenetrates the body also, but concentrates around the brain or head area. The *'Uhane* cannot extend any portion of its ***aka*** body outward. The *'Uhane* exerts the energy or *mana* of its Will through its ***aka*** body. The **entire** ***aka*** body of the *'Uhane* can disconnect from the physical body and go astral traveling. Some people believe that the *'Uhane* travels to the land of Spirit in its ***aka*** body when we dream. Both Selves that reside in the physical body travel outside the physical body using their ***aka*** bodies leaving a connecting ***aka*** cord attached so they can easily return to the physical body or *kino*. The ***aka*** bodies of the *'Uhane* and the *'Unihipili* are the luminous energies captured on film by Kirlian and aura photography.

THE LIGHT BODY OF THE *'AUMAKUA*

The body of the *'Aumakua* is not made of ***aka*** substance, which only functions on the physical plane. We do not know what kind of body the *'Aumakua* actually has, but it has been described as a body made of light that our human eyes cannot penetrate. Often people report seeing their Guardian Angel or *'Aumakua* as a magnificent ball of blue-white light, surrounded by a brilliant yellow-white light that radiates a great feeling of love. People, who have had near-death experiences, also describe these Light Beings. The halos extending around the heads of saints and other religious figures in early paintings are symbolic of the light body of the *'Aumakua* hovering around its charge.

> The *'Aumakua* uses the connecting ***aka*** cord to return energy to its person in the form of blessings. It also transmits inspirations, visions, intuitions and feelings of love, patience, and compassion, (all the Divine feelings), to the two Selves residing in the physical body along this ***aka*** cord.

The ***aka*** cords between the three selves are strengthened each time contact is made. The thicker the braided ***aka*** cord becomes, the stronger the connection between the Selves. It is through the ***aka*** cord connecting the *'Unihipili* and the *'Aumakua* that prayer requests are sent. It is through this ***aka*** cord that premonitions, intuitions, visions, dreams and inspirations are transmitted from the *'Aumakua* to the *'Unihipili*, who may or may not share them with the *'Uhane*.

Knots can form in the ***aka*** cord connecting the *'Unihipili* and the *'Aumakua,* blocking the path between them. These knots or blocks are the guilts, complexes and fixations lodged in the ***aka*** body of the *'Unihipili*. In order to clear the path to the High Self, these knots must be cleared from the *'Unihipili*. If the knots are not cleared away, communication, prayers and guidance cannot flow between the Selves.

INNERACTIVITY

Purpose: To consciously experience the reaching out of the *'Unihipili* along the *aka* threads.

This is a game you might have played as a child. Pick a partner and decide which one will be the "guesser" and which one will be "it." The person who is "it" takes an object that can be hidden completely in a closed hand and places both his or her own hands behind the back, placing the object in one hand or the other without showing the "guesser." After the object is hidden, bring both hands around to the front so that the "guesser" can choose in which hand the object is hidden. The "guesser" **first** asks his or her *'Unihipili* to extend an *aka* finger to determine the hand in which the object is hidden. Make the guess based on the response of the *'Unihipili*. (Pay close attention to what is happening inside your mind and inside your solar plexus. Take time to listen before making the choice.) After three turns of choosing, the "guesser" becomes "it" and the game begins again.

(Take a few minutes to write down anything that you wish to remember about this **Inneractivity**. Were you able to feel any sensations before the choice was made? Did you find that your *'Uhane* overrode the first choice of your *'Unihipili*? How many times did you choose correctly? Was there any resistance to playing this game?)

Personal comments:

CONTINUING INNERACTIVITY

Purpose: To strengthen the psychic connection between the *'Unihipili* and the *'Uhane.*

There are all kinds of ways in which you can explore the expertise of your *'Unihipili* in the use of its *aka* body. The *'Unihipili* loves to play games and will cooperate if you make the explorations fun. Before you play any game, ask if your *'Unihipili* would like to play and remember to thank it for playing when the game ends. Remember to stop playing if the *'Unihipili* becomes tired or bored. You can try again another day. Examples of different kinds of *aka* games are to:

1. Find a parking place in advance.

2. Find lost objects.

3. Play the children's card game called "Concentration." Place all the cards face down on the table and guess the location of the cards to make pairs.

4. Use the telephone book to locate a certain object you need by checking which store has the object.

5. Play any kind of game where something is hidden, i.e., small objects placed in covered boxes or sealed bags.

Be creative in playing these ***aka*** games. The more you play, the stronger the psychic connection between your *'Unihipili* and *'Uhane* becomes. When the connection becomes very strong, your *'Unihipili* will begin to share with your *'Uhane* more information about situations or people using more than your five physical senses.

Continuing Personal Comments:

THE THREE ENERGIES OR VITAL FORCES (*MANA*)

Mana is a form of energy that has strong electro-magnetic qualities. ***Mana*** can take the form of magnetism and be stored in wood and other porous substances. In the middle 1700's, Franz Anton Mesmer demonstrated the magnetic quality of ***mana*** when he charged iron rods, water, and trees for the purpose of transferring this energy to heal his clients. He was quite a successful healer. One of the side effects of mesmerism was the strong volt of ***mana*** that knocked some people unconscious. Surgeons used this method of inducing unconsciousness in their patients before the discovery of ether and hypnosis.

In times of war in ancient Hawai'i, certain *Kahuna,* adept in generating and transferring energy, transferred their ***mana*** to throwing sticks. During battle, the *Kahuna* threw the *mana*-charged sticks over the heads of his warriors towards the opposing side. If an enemy warrior was struck by the stick or even if he were close to the stick when it landed, the *mana* would discharge and the warrior would fall to the ground unconscious.

"*Mana* responds to the commands and directions of the consciousness of sentient beings," according to Long. The *'Unihipili* transforms and directs the ***mana*** as the energy for charging the physical body processes. The *'Uhane* transforms and directs the ***mana-mana*** in the thought process. The ***mana-mana*** of the *'Uhane* cannot travel over the *aka* threads unless a thought form goes with it to be planted as a suggestion. The *'Aumakua* commands the ***mana-loa*** in the process of creation, transmuting matter in a way we do not yet understand. The *'Uhane* can also direct the *'Unihipili* to use a surcharge of ***mana*** for other purposes. For example, during the healing process known as "laying on of hands," a surcharge of ***mana*** is directed to stimulate the body towards healing.

> ***MANA*** **RESPONDS TO THE DIRECTIONS OF CONSCIOUSNESS.**

The ***mana-loa*** of the *'Aumakua* is that of the atom-splitting variety. The power of creation is something scientists are striving to understand. This energy, ***mana-loa***, can be combined with the ***mana-loa*** of other *'Aumakua* to bring about shifts in larger physical matter. ***Mana-loa*** can also be stored in natural objects, such as stone or wood, which can then be tapped for healing. The *'Aumakua* must have a sufficient amount of earthly ***mana*** to effect changes in dense physical matter.

The *'Aumakua* regularly contacts its person during sleep when the *'Unihipili* gives it the ***mana*** it needs to create on the physical level. The other two Selves can also come together to send a deliberate, conscious gift of **energy** to the *'Aumakua.* The real meaning behind the offering of a "sacrifice," is the offering of ***mana*** to the High Self. To fully activate the trinity of humanness, ***mana*** is offered on a daily basis to the *'Aumakua.* Each prayer, in order to be answered, needs a surcharge of ***mana*** sent with it.

EVERY PRAYER NEEDS A SURCHARGE OF *MANA* SENT WITH IT.

The symbol for ***mana*** in *Hawai'ian,* and in other ancient cultures as well, is "water" or *"wai."* The energy or ***mana*** should be in a continuous balanced flow from the *'Aumakua* to the *'Unihipili* to the *'Uhane* and back. The symbols of the ***mana-loa*** of the *'Aumakua* returning to its person are clouds and mist made up of fine droplets of water. *Mana,* when falling in the form of fine rain, symbolizes the return of vital force as a blessing to help and heal the other Selves.

***MANA* FROM THE HIGH SELF IS SYMBOLIZED BY CLOUDS AND MIST FALLING AS FINE RAIN.**

The symbol for the ***mana*** rising up from the *'Unihipili* to the *'Aumakua* is water rising upward and overflowing as in a fountain. The symbol in India of the Kundalini energy rising up from the base of the spine along the spinal column up through the top of the head is also symbolic of the rising of the *mana. Mana* is called "prana" in India.

***MANA* RISING FROM THE *'UNIHIPILI* TO THE HIGH SELF IS SYMBOLIZED AS WATER RISING UPWARD AND OVERFLOWING AS IN A FOUNTAIN.**

Mana also means "strength," "power," "intelligence," and "divided or branching out." The *Hawai'ian* word for thinking is *"mana-o."* This literally means "something done with ***mana***." The word for miracle is *"hana mana,"* which means " to work, labor, duty, to develop as a picture, and to create heat [energy]."

HOW TO GENERATE *MANA*

Mana is generated or accumulated in several ways:

- Through awareness and direction of thoughts;
- Creative visualization;
- Feeling strong emotions;
- Consciously breathing;
- Physical exercise;
- Speaking powerful words;
- Tapping into the energy of nature.

The *'Unihipili* generates ***mana*** through the action of oxygenating and raising the sugar level in the blood. A normal charge of ***mana*** is needed to keep the body in good working condition. We pick up extra ***mana*** from the universal source by tapping into the wellspring of energy that permeates the physical plane.

The *'Uhane* can direct the *'Unihipili* to accumulate ***mana*** and store it for specific purposes. James Redfield, author of *The Celestine Prophecy,* suggests an exercise for tapping into the energy of nature. Find a place of beauty and become aware of the energy fields surrounding every element of nature. Consciously set up a continuous energy flow between yourself and the natural beauty around you. This is a good way to revitalize and experience the natural exchange of energy of the physical world. (Note: James Redfield does not use the term ***mana*** in his book.)

There are other ways to accumulate ***mana***. Your *'Uhane* can use its powers of imagination and consciously picture the energy growing with an appropriate symbol. The ancient *Kahuna* used the symbol or picture of water rising up as in a fountain. The *'Unihipili* knows automatically what the image is to create and you will feel the ***mana*** rising almost immediately. Stop for a moment and visualize water rising up in a fountain and notice that your body begins to warm and you feel the ***mana*** rising.

Strong emotions can also create ***mana*** by activating the breathing that increases your energy. When you feel a strong emotion, you feel more energetic, no matter what the emotion is. It could be anger or fear or love or joy. Remember that emotions follow thought and the *'Uhane* can aid the *'Unihipili* by asking for certain situations or feelings to be brought to its conscious attention. From these thoughts the emotions flow and thus create the energy or ***mana***. Practice generating ***mana*** from joyous or loving thoughts so you do not reinforce any negative patterns in your *'Unihipili.*

Deliberate breathing in a slow rhythmic pattern creates a surcharge of ***mana*** without having to engage the emotions. The *Hawai'ian* word for breath is *"ha."* It also stands for the number "four." Long developed what he calls "The *Ha* Rite" to use the breath in a prayer ritual to create ***mana*** to send to the *'Aumakua*. (The *Ha* Rite is discussed in a later section.)

"*HA*" MEANS BREATH OR FOUR.

When the missionaries first came to *Hawai'i* the natives believed the missionaries could heal the sick as their *Bible* stated. The *Hawai'ians* brought their ill and lame to the missionaries for healing, but the missionaries only uttered a few words of prayer over them and the sick were not healed. The *Hawai'ians* knew you had to "breathe life into your prayers," so they called the foreigners *"ha'oles,"* which means "those without breath."

There is a story told by Mother Alice *Kahokuoluna* of Hawaiʻi, who was the pastor of the first Protestant church built on the Island of Molokaʻ*i*. Her church was named "The Church of the Healing Spring." (The term "Mother" is the Hawaiʻian title of respect given to Rev. *Kahokuoluna*.) This story is told in *Strengthening the Spiritual Life,* by Dr. Nels Ferre.

> "Before the missionaries came, my people used to sit outside their temples for a long time meditating and preparing themselves before entering. Then they would virtually creep to the altar to offer their petition and afterwards would again sit a long time outside, this time to "breathe life" into their prayers. The Christians, when they came, just got up, uttered a few sentences, said Amen and were done. For that reason my people called them "ha'oles, "without breath" or "those who failed to breathe life into their prayers."

The *ʻUhane* is the one who directs the *ʻUnihipili* to deliberately begin to breathe and to accumulate an extra charge of ***mana***. It does this with its Will or intention. Just thinking about breathing deeply and regularly will start the process. The *ʻUnihipili* already knows how to do it and has been listening to these instructions. Try this for yourself. Think about breathing deeply and notice that your breathing is beginning to slow and deepen. When accumulating ***mana*** with the breath, you don't want to hyperventilate. Pause now and then to breathe regularly. Ask your *ʻUnihipili* to collect and store the ***mana*** until you direct its use. If you are practicing any of these exercises and have a surcharge of ***mana***, send it to your *ʻAumakua* as a gift of love.

SEND ANY EXTRA *MANA* YOU GENERATE TO YOUR *ʻAUMAKUA* AS A GIFT OF LOVE.

Mana is generated more powerfully in a group. It is not just doubled, but increases exponentially. The uplifting feeling of energy experienced during certain emotional religious ceremonies is an example of the increased power of group ***mana***. The priests and priestesses of all the world's religions know the power of this increased ***mana***. They use it to perform rituals to request healings and blessings for the people in their care.

MANA CAN BE GENERATED MORE POWERFULLY IN A GROUP.

There are different ways to increase and use group ***mana***. A good example of group mana is the *Dances of Universal Peace*. The Sufis teach people worldwide how to increase, hold, and use their energy to help establish world peace. The dancers build the ***mana*** by participating in the dancing and singing. Drums and other musical instruments are also used to impress the □*Unihipili* and encourage them to generate ***mana***. At the end of each dance the dancers pause and hold the energy they have just generated. Then they release it to bless the world with peace. The dances are representative of the sacred teachings of every nation, thus respecting and honoring the beliefs of all people, an important ingredient for establishing world peace. Sacred dance is used in many cultures for generating group energy.

It is important to keep your *mana* balanced as Dr. Otha Wingo, explains in his audiotape entitled, "The Huna Way to Effective Living." We are continually bombarded with discordant energies in our culture. Air conditioning, appliances, fluorescent lights, microwaves and any number of other energy producing items affect us. He explains that the '*Uhane* continually filters the sensory receptors to avoid the full impact of outside stimuli and it takes a lot of energy or ***mana*** to do this. He suggests a simple exercise to restore balance to your energy. Take a few minutes and lightly touch the fingertips of one hand to the fingertips of your other hand and hold this position until you feel more balanced.

It is important to keep your *mana* balanced.

Dr. Wingo also suggests that our society is designed to block the flow of energy and we should practice balancing techniques daily to keep our energy flowing freely. We should think about it regularly and always work from a surcharge of energy or ***mana*** so we do not become depleted.

Whenever you are feeling out of energy, tired, sad or listless, direct a surcharge of ***mana*** to be gathered and use it to invigorate your body. ***Mana*** can also be used to bring the mind back to alertness. ***Mana*** is one of your greatest personal resources and you should learn how to accumulate it and use it daily.

***MANA* IS ONE OF YOUR GREATEST PERSONAL RESOURCES.**

USE SOME EVERY DAY.

INNERACTIVITY

Purpose: To experience the presence of *mana* within the body.

THE STAR EXERCISE

(This exercise was taught to Max Freedom Long by Baron Eugene Ferson.)

Stand tall with your feet wide apart. Extend your arms to the side, level with your shoulders. Turn your left palm face up and your right palm face down. You are forming your body into a five-pointed star. Raise your eyes to the Heavens. Maintain this position and repeat the following affirmation with conviction:

"Universal Life Energy is flowing through me. I feel it NOW!"

Repeat this aloud slowly four times pausing about 20 seconds between repetitions. Expect to accumulate a surcharge of ***mana***. Be aware of any tingling or prickling sensations in the palms of your hands or in your wrists that indicate the building up of the extra charge of ***mana***. Put your hands on your thymus area and direct the ***mana*** to go to your body.

The more you practice the Star Exercise the better your *'Unihipili* will become at generating energy just by saying the affirmation silently to yourself.

(Take a few minutes to write down anything that you want to remember about this **Inneractivity**. Could you feel the ***mana*** in your hands or wrists? Was it difficult to repeat the affirmation with conviction?)

Personal Comments:

INNERACTIVITY

Purpose: To measure the amount of extra *mana* that can be accumulated by your *'Unihipili.*

The Pendulum Method

(Based on an exercise by Max Long)

The pendulum is a great tool for communication between your *'Uhane* and your *'Unihipili.* Dowsers use it to locate water and other items. Some healers use it to diagnose and prescribe medicines. Your *'Unihipili* moves the pendulum with the involuntary muscles of the physical body. This **Inneractivity** is an introduction to the use of the pendulum as a tool for measuring ***mana***.

1. Using the hand that is most comfortable for you, suspend the pendulum between the thumb and index finger. Place your other hand palm up and open underneath the suspended pendulum.

2. Say out loud to your *'Unihipili* that you want to measure the amount of ***mana*** that is currently in your body and then wait.

3. The pendulum will begin to either circle or swing back and forth. It doesn't matter which response you get. The idea is to count either the number of circles or the number of swings before the pendulum slows down and stops. The initial number of circles or swings your *'Unihipili* shows you is not important. You want to establish a base line measuring the energy in your body. The purpose of this exercise is to measure the difference between your normal charge of ***mana*** and a surcharge of ***mana***.

Record the base number here: __________

4. Now ask your *'Unihipili* to accumulate a surcharge of ***mana***, using any method you like. Direct your *'Unihipili* to store this ***mana*** so that it can be measured.

5. Take up the pendulum again as before and direct your *'Unihipili* out loud to measure the surcharge of ***mana*** you have just accumulated and count the circles or swings.

Record this number here: __________

6. The second measurement should be more than the first measurement. Use this method to determine, if you are unsure, whether your *'Unihipili* has accumulated a surcharge of ***mana*** or not.

You can establish your normal count by doing this exercise over a several days. Don't try to establish your normal count by repeating this exercise over and over on the same day. The *'Unihipili* becomes bored of any game that ceases to be fun.

(Take a few minutes to write down anything that you want to remember about this **Inneractivity**. Did your *'Unihipili* cooperate with you? Was it easy for you to accumulate a surcharge of ***mana***? Were you able to accumulate a large or small surcharge of ***mana***?)

Personal Comments:

CONTINUING INNERACTIVTY

Purpose: To increase your health by using *mana*.

With the cooperation of your *'Unihipili* you can use ***mana*** to increase both your physical health and your mental health. First request the cooperation of your *'Unihipili* in accumulating a surcharge of ***mana*** and direct it to the area that needs healing.

To increase your physical health or invigorate your body during periods of tiredness or fatigue:

1. Find a quiet place where you won't be disturbed for a few minutes. Ask your *'Unihipili* to accumulate a surcharge of ***mana***. Take deep breaths and visualize the ***mana*** increasing. Continue breathing until you feel you have accumulated enough ***mana***.

2. Hold the ***mana*** in readiness and direct your *'Unihipili* to send the ***mana*** to your body or any part of your body that needs extra energy or healing. Picture and feel this ***mana*** flowing into and through every cell in your body, revitalizing and renewing. Put your hands over any part that needs extra energy as you send the *mana* into your body.

3. When you feel all the extra ***mana*** has been discharged, thank your *'Unihipili* for its help and return to whatever you were doing

When you are mentally tired, you can revitalize your mind by following the above steps, substituting your mind as the receiver of the extra ***mana***. This works very well when you are in the middle of a project that takes a lot of mental energy. It works well when you are studying, taking a test or any time you need a surcharge of mental energy.

Continuing Personal Comments:

COMMUNICATION BETWEEN THE 'UHANE AND THE 'UNIHIPILI

Communication between the *'Uhane* and the *'Unihipili* is something we do all the time, but it is often like the communication in dysfunctional families. Dysfunctional family members develop negative habits of talking with each other, often using outrageous methods to get their own ways. This causes the other members of the family to respond in kind. Like dysfunctional family members, our subconscious and our conscious minds develop outrageous methods of communication and often fail at the very basics.

For example, how many times a day, through our thoughts or spoken words, do we attack ourselves or downgrade ourselves? How often do we undermine our own self-esteem? How many times do we make up our mind to do something and find that we can't, or haven't, for some obscure reason? Why do we often feel like we are just "treading water," never really getting anywhere? Why do we find ourselves mired down day after day in the bog of indecision and inner conflict? These are examples of the problems that occur because we do not have the trust and rapport between the Selves necessary for basic communication.

HOW GOOD IS OUR INNER COMMUNICATION?

Our lack of effective communication keeps us from tapping into the natural resources of each of the Selves and inhibits us from developing our inner power and becoming whole. But there is a way we can change the old patterns of ineffective communication, build trust and rapport between the Selves, and claim our power!

***HUNA* HELPS US BUILD BETTER COMMUNICATION BETWEEN THE SELVES.**

How do we accomplish this? By practicing the principles of ***Huna*** on a daily basis. ***Huna*** gives us the most practical and effective methods to build a better inner communication system. First, acknowledge that you have a thinking Self (*'Uhane*) and a feeling Self (*'Unihipili*). Realize that you posses two separate kinds of awareness. Both are valid ways of perceiving the physical world and reacting to it.

Second, begin to distinguish the difference between thinking and feeling (logic and emotion) and validate each process. There is a subtle change when the thinking self (*'Uhane*) takes over from the feeling self (*'Unihipili*) and vice versa. To recognize this change is one of the first steps in establishing communication. Know which part of you is communicating and how the communication is taking place. It is probably easier for most of us to recognize when the *'Uhane* is in control, since we are most often aware we are thinking.

ACKNOWLEDGE THAT COMMUNICATION IS MORE THAN JUST WORDS.

Third, listen to your own inner dialogue and become an observer of the process. Learn how your *'Uhane* and *'Unihipili* communicate with each other and note the areas in which you could make improvements. This is part of the process. Dr. Donald H. Schuster in his book, *Huna: A Magic Way of Life,* suggests that tactile sensations are a way to begin to learn to communicate with your Selves. The *'Unihipili* communicates with the *'Uhane* through these sensations, such as itches. For example, if you would like to check to see if you have open communication with your own *'Unihipili,* start washing dishes and notice if any itches appear on your face that you can't scratch because of your wet hands. If an itch appears, you have a problem in communication with your *'Unihipili.* Itches are also indications of other specific problems, depending on their locations.

OBSERVE YOUR OWN INNER DIALOGUE

Fourth, affirm your desire to establish better communication and ask the cooperation of each Self to be open, non-judgmental, trusting and trustworthy, and to always act out of love, honor and respect for the other. Make a covenant, a "contractual spiritual relationship," as James Alexander calls it, with your selves to speak the truth to one another. Essentially you become your own best friends always loving and caring for each other.

MAKE A COVENANT WITH YOUR SELF.

INNERACTIVITY

Purpose: To differentiate between the two Selves and begin the process of communication.

Color Meditation

(Based on an exercise developed by Ann Ree Colton.)

This **Inneractivity** is a color meditation in which you allow both Selves to participate as individuals and enjoy what you have created together. You will need a blank sheet of paper and colored chalk. **In this exercise do not try to make a picture using your conscious mind.**

From the awareness of your *'Uhane* assume an attitude of meditation and close your eyes. Quiet your mind and then quiet your body. Lovingly invite your *'Unihipili* to join you in this **Inneractivity**. When your mind and body are quiet and you have a feeling of cooperation from your *'Unihipili*, open your eyes and select a piece of colored chalk based on a feeling. Take the chalk and, meditatively and deliberately, completely cover the entire surface of the blank sheet of paper. It doesn't matter which direction you make the marks, but be sure to cover the entire page. Be in the moment and enjoy the feel of the chalk in your hand and the beauty of the color as it fills up the empty paper. Do not try to draw a picture or any form, simply cover the entire paper with color.

When you are finished with the first color, put the chalk down and quietly look at the paper. As you look at your colored paper, pictures and images begin to appear. Select another piece of colored chalk, letting your feelings guide you, and outline the pictures and images as they appear. Sometimes you will see many small pictures or images. Other times you will see one larger picture with smaller details. Don't try to analyze this process. Let the images appear as they will. You may want to turn the paper different directions to see more images. Keep outlining until you feel you are finished and then put the chalk and the paper down.

Close your eyes once again and quiet the mind and the body. Thank your *'Unihipili* for its help in creating this experience and assure it that you will have many more enjoyable experiences together in the future. When you are ready, open your eyes and look at your picture once more. You will find a special message on your paper from your *'Unihipili* to your *'Uhane* in the form of the pictures and images you have outlined.

Give your meditation paper a title that both your *'Uhane* and the *'Unihipili* agree upon. Keep your creation in a prominent place for a week and see if any other messages come to your *'Uhane* from your *'Unihipili*. A good place to display your picture is on your refrigerator or mirror.

(Take a few minutes and write down anything that you want to remember from this **Inneractivity**. Did your *'Unihipili* enjoy coloring? Did your *'Uhane* want to control the whole process? Did you learn anything new about your *'Unihipili*?)

Personal Comments:

CONTINUING INNERACTIVITY

Purpose: To experience the presence of your three Selves by inviting the *'Aumakua* to join in as you continue the color meditations.

Follow the steps outlined above to prepare for the meditation. When you invite your *'Unihipili* to participate, take a few minutes and also invite your *'Aumakua* to participate. When the *'Aumakua* joins the other two Selves, the content of the meditation pictures become more spiritual and the messages more inspirational. Keep your color meditations in a portfolio and look at them often to remind yourself of how it feels to have all your Selves working together as a whole. Spray your pictures with hair spray or a fixative to preserve them.

Continuing Personal Comments:

TRAINING THE TWO SELVES THAT RESIDE IN THE *KINO*

Our purpose on this earth is to evolve both physically and spiritually. Based on the ***Huna*** model, we have two earthly minds or "souls" or Selves that need to grow and learn. How do we train ourselves to develop those qualities of each Self that fulfills right purpose and brings out the Divine in each? The following section outlines ways to train both the *'Uhane* and the *'Unihipili.*

TRAINING THE *'UHANE*

When your awareness is in your mind, you are in the awareness of the ***'Uhane***. Whenever you are speaking, you are in the awareness of your ***'Uhane***. The development of the Will; the control of obsessive or negative thoughts and words; the development of strong moral guidelines based on a life of "no hurt;" and, the uplifting of the consciousness of the mind through the practice of love are important areas of growth for the ***'Uhane***. There comes a time in all our lives when we must take on the responsibility for the actions of our mind. This is a very critical step in our mature development.

> **WE MUST TAKE ON THE RESPONSIBILITY FOR THE ACTIONS OF OUR OWN MIND.**

THE DEVELOPMENT OF THE WILL

The use of the Will is the most important ability inherent in the *'Uhane*. It is through the development of the Will that the *'Uhane* takes its rightful place in the human trinity. William James, the great American philosopher, said that the fundamental faculty of the Will is a capacity to *direct our attention.* This is done through the use of thought reinforced by *mana-mana*. You experience the use of your Will all the time. Whenever you plan a goal and attain that goal, the process you used in getting there utilized your Will. It was the force that made you choose certain activities to reach your goal rather than other activities that did not relate to your goal. It is that force that directs your attention to a specific purpose. It is the director of both inner and outer changes. The Will helps us to synthesize and harmonize.

> **ATTENTION IS THOUGHT REINFORCED WITH *MANA-MANA*.**

> **QUALITIES OF THE WILL:**
>
> - **ACTIVE PRINCIPLE**
> - **INDIVIDUALIZER**
> - **CHOOSER**
> - **AGENT OF OBEDIENCE**
> - **CHANGER**
> - **OPPOSER OF MIND**
> - **DEVELOPER**
> - **MOTIVATOR**
> - **GUIDE**

In his book, *Paradox of Power,* Mark Thurston discusses the Will and how your Will moves you from an idea to an act. He quotes nine principles taken from the readings of Edgar Cayce that describe the qualities of the Will.

As an active principle, the Will participates in our growth and evolution. As an individualizer, the Will makes us unique and gives us the ability to create. The Will allows us to select among alternative courses of actions as the chooser. As an agent of obedience, the Will allows forces beyond our own personal sphere to influence us and as a changer, we reshape our lives through our Will. As the opposer of mind, the Will stands as the control mechanism over the body (in ***Huna*** the *'Unihipili*). As the developer, the Will is the heart of our spiritual growth and as the motivator, it moves us towards our goals. As the guide, the Will assists the mind (in ***Huna*** the ***'Uhane***) to lead the life that supports and nourishes the best in us.

> **THE WILL IS FULLY OPERATIONAL BY AGE 12.**

The Will of the ***'Uhane*** begins to develop at about age 2 and is normally fully operational by age 12. The ability for self-control is a sign that the ***'Uhane*** has taken over control of the direction of the life of the person on the physical plane. From this stage and throughout the rest of life, the Will of the ***'Uhane*** is a primary resource for the development of the human being.

> **A HEALTHY WILL MANIFESTS SELF-DISCIPLINE AND SELF-CONTROL.**

A healthy Will manifests self-discipline and self-control. It gives us "courageous initiative" to start new things. It is the mediator between the past, present and future. Our Will can alter every condition based upon our past. Our Will can invigorate every condition based upon our future. Our Will produces "visionary imagination" and draws us toward that which we are to become.

There are certain stages to the development of the Will as explained by Thurston. The first stage is the Sleeping Will. This is the condition of the Will from birth to age 6. The next stage is the Distinguishing Will, which is the beginning of the ability to self-identify and separate the ***'Uhane*** from the *'Unihipili.* The next stage is the Skillful Will, where a person achieves an inner split, the awareness of the distinction of thoughts from feelings or the ***'Uhane*** from the *'Unihipili.*

SLEEPING WILL | **DISTINGUISHING WILL** | **SKILLFUL WILL**

EMPOWERING WILL | **TRANSPERSONAL WILL**

The next stage is the Empowering Will, which is the developing of the awareness that there is more to life than the physical properties. This is also the time when we recognize that the world, which is presented by the *'Unihipili*, is not the present, but the past. This is the stage where we recognize our potential to become the Ideal Human.

The final stage is the Transpersonal Will, where we learn to align ourselves with the Divine and cleanse the negative patterns from our lives. It is the stage where the authentic person emerges as the path to the High Self or *'Aumakua* is cleared. It is the stage where the intuition, inspiration, and creativity of the *'Aumakua* flows freely into the life of the other two Selves and we awaken to our full creative potential.

TECHNIQUES FOR AWAKENING THE WILL

1. The first technique for awakening the Will is **MEDITATION**. It doesn't matter which method you use for meditation. The important part is to do it on a daily basis and to learn to quiet the mind. The ***'Uhane*** becomes so caught up in its own thoughts, and the process of calling them up from the *'Unihipili*, that it forgets to be quiet. It is through this quietness of mind that the presence of the *'Aumakua* is truly known. Long describes meditation as the process of moving into the level of the *'Unihipili* and quieting the memory-retrieving process. When this is accomplished and the *'Unihipili* is at rest, you move into the level of the *'Aumakua* and feel the presence of the High Self.

2. The second technique is **ENGAGING SELF-OBSERVATION**. G. I. Gurdjieff, a Russian born teacher of spiritual development, first proposed this technique. In this practice, you make a conscious effort to separate your ***'Uhane*** and stand aside from your *'Unihipili* to observe old habit patterns. Make no judgments when observing these patterns. When your ***'Uhane*** focuses its attention on the pattern and determines how and when it arises, then it is time to communicate with your *'Unihipili* about the old pattern. The object of the practice is to observe the pattern, discuss the pattern with your *'Unihipili* and together make a determination as to whether the continued pattern is helpful or hurtful to the Selves.

3. The third technique is **VISIONARY SELF-CONTROL**. This practice promotes self-discipline through affirmation rather than through negation. Self-control and self-discipline are more effective when linked to a vision or a personal ideal. The duty of the ***'Uhane*** is to develop and maintain a strong personal moral guideline for all actions of the two Selves. When your *'Unihipili* presents a desire, drive or appetite that your ***'Uhane*** deems inappropriate to the higher personal ideal, you **acknowledge** the value of the desire and **confirm** that the satisfaction of the desire will be given an appropriate outlet and time. In other words, repression is not in the best interest of self-discipline. The desire is *acknowledged* as valued and appreciated rather than *repressed* or *judged unworthy*. The satisfaction of the desire is then changed to an affirmative action that expresses the personal vision or personal ideal.

Using positive affirmations such as "let's do take time to meditate " or "let's do take time to play" are ways of using this technique. Write and speak your affirmations with positive words. Daily use of affirmations is important. Affirmations are more effective when charged with *mana*. Take a few deep breaths before saying the affirmations out loud. This extra charge of *mana* will reinforce the suggestions of the affirmations in the *'Unihipili*.

4. **TEACHING AND GIVING LOVE** with every response to a situation is the fourth technique for training the ***'Uhane***. Control the normal reactions to situations by directing responses in an affirmative way, empowered with love. This takes a conscious effort. This is the practice of extending your loving Will. This technique is practiced on yourself, as well as others, until it becomes a positive habit of mind. Start by recognizing when you want to respond to a situation with negativity and change that response to one of love. For example, "road rage" is a major problem on our highways. Instead of getting angry with the people who cut in front of you, acknowledge the improper act without judgment and send the other driver on his or her way with a blessing for a safe and happy journey.

5. The fifth technique is **HARMONIZING SYNTHESIS.** In this technique, your ***'Uhane*** focuses its intent on inclusive resolution or "win-win solutions." When a conflict of any kind arises, set your intention to make winners of all parties involved. Another part of this practice is to acknowledge your part in a negative situation and offer your help to figure out a way to make it better. In other words, begin to change your feelings of being hurt or defensive to feelings of worthiness and helpfulness.

All of these techniques for training the Will of the *'Uhane* help discover opportunities to express the talents and potentialities of both the *'Unihipili* and the *'Uhane.*

INNERACTIVITY

Purpose: To awaken the Will by demonstrating mutual resolution possibilities using HARMONIZING SYNTHESIS.

This **Inneractivity** lifts the consciousness of the minds of the participants to a higher level, to that level where we are all connected, **for what happens to you happens to me.** This technique involves the use of creative thinking, exploring the endless possibilities of new ideas and resolutions to bring harmony and love into our life.

Sit across the table from a partner. Put your right elbows on the table in front of you and grasp hands firmly. The object is to see how many times you can win at arm wrestling and how many times your partner can win at arm wrestling in one minute.

List the combined number here _________

(Take a few minutes and write down anything that you want to remember about this **Inneractivity**. When did you realize that both parties could win? Was it easy to move from the level of competition to the level of cooperation?)

Personal Comments:

CONTINUING INNERACTIVITY

Purpose: To choose and refine your spiritual ideal.

(This exercise is based on Mark Thurston's exercises in *Paradox of Power*, and the work of Psychology Professor Mihaly Csikszentmihalyi.)

In order to attain the kind of life we desire, we must have a "life theme, a central purpose toward which we continue to flow." When we are in the flow, everything seems right. Being in the flow does not necessarily mean life is easy, but we feel completely confident, capable and happy. This theme must have clear objectives, clear rules for action, and a way for both Selves to concentrate and become involved. Knowing our life theme brings us closer to the optimal experience of being human, where we can enjoy true happiness. Our *'Uhane* formulates our life theme with the emotional input from our *'Unihipili.*

Use your own personal process to center yourself. When you are centered, stay in the awareness of your *'Uhane* and write the answers to the following questions.

1. What human qualities do I value most? (honesty, peace, love, etc.)

2. When I am my "best self," in what direction do I want my life to go?

3. Using the answers to the above questions, write down a single word or short phrase that best describes your life theme.

Write down your phrase on a piece of paper and attach it to your refrigerator or other visible place where you can read it every day. When it no longer best describes your present spiritual ideal, do the **Inneractivity** again and revise it.

Continuing Personal Comments:

TRAINING THE *'UNIHIPILI*

The *'Uhane* stands as teacher and guide to the ***'Unihipili.*** It is the older and wiser Sister or Brother. This does not mean that the *'Uhane* is a parent and the ***'Unihipili*** is its child. But rather there is a spirit of love and cooperation between the Selves. They honor and respect each other. Each Self depends on the abilities and talents of the other Self to function. Together they are more powerful and have a greater capacity to grow and develop.

Training the ***'Unihipili*** is one of the primary duties of the *'Uhane* and one that cannot be disregarded or ignored. Just as the *'Aumakua* will not, and cannot, leave the two Selves without loving assistance, your *'Uhane* cannot leave your ***'Unihipili***. Training the ***'Unihipili*** is a continuous process. Frequent review and repetition are the basics of good teaching. If you make the learning fun, your ***'Unihipili*** will more readily cooperate. Remember to quit when your ***'Unihipili*** becomes tired. There is always another time, another day, for this is a life long task. As your *'Uhane* learns and grows, it passes on new knowledge to your ***'Unihipili*** for they both must be ready to graduate together.

REMEMBER TO MAKE LEARNING FUN.

TECHNIQUES FOR TEACHING THE *'UNIHIPILI*

1. The first technique is **COMMUNICATION.** Learn how to communicate with your ***'Unihipili.*** Honor and acknowledge the ***'Unihipili*** as a part of yourself. A good way to begin is to find out his or her name. This is not as easy as it sounds. Some ***'Unihipili*** will quickly disclose his or her name, but others require patience, persistence and reassurance that the *'Uhane* is serious about learning to communicate. This name isn't a name your *'Uhane* chooses, but is chosen by your ***'Unihipili.*** How will you know the true name? You will have a strong feeling of rightness inside when the name is spoken out loud. Your ***'Unihipili's*** name should reflect dignity, pride and self-worth. (Pet names such as "Noodles" or "Dum-Dum" are not appropriate.) Learning to communicate by using the pendulum is helpful in this first technique. The process of learning the name of your ***'Unihipili*** is as important as the name itself.

Another form of communication is dreams. The ***'Unihipili*** uses images and symbols to communicate – the stuff of which dreams are made. Keep a dream journal of your dreams or fragments of dreams. Write down both your logical and emotional interpretation of each dream. This is an excellent way to learn the language of your own ***'Unihipili.*** Remember the language of the *'Unihipili* is symbols. Look for symbols in your every day life.

2. The second technique is **BUILDING LOVE AND TRUST.** There must be love and trust between the Selves. Our ***'Unihipili*** is talking to us all the time trying to tell us all sorts of things we need to know, but we rarely listen. Most often we ignore our inner Sister or Brother to the point where he or she ceases to tell us anything. That "still, small voice" is not really our conscience, but our ***'Unihipili*** talking to us. That voice is often so small it takes a real effort to hear it. In this technique we build love and trust by learning to listen to the inner feelings of the ***'Unihipili.*** And we must learn to listen without judging. Many modern teachings urge us to stop judging our fellow humans, but forget about not judging ourselves. We first learn to stop judging our ***'Unihipili*** and then we learn to stop judging others.

As the judgments stop, your *'**Unihipili*** becomes more trusting and begins to cooperate as it should. When you find yourself thinking, reacting to, or voicing judgments such as, "I'm really stupid for doing that," or "What a jerk I was!" stop immediately and talk to your *'**Unihipili.*** Apologize for the incorrect remark (remember words carry power) and emphasize that you, the *'Uhane*, do not believe that your *'**Unihipili*** is "stupid" or a "jerk." Say to yourself that you believe your *'**Unihipili*** to be extremely smart and capable, and most importantly that you love your *'**Unihipili*** no matter what. **Do not underestimate the value of this practice.** Do it every time you give yourself negative thoughts or negative talk.

The Japanese scientist Masaru Emoto has proven in the laboratory that positive and negative words and energy affect the physical body. He exposed samples of water to different words, phrases and music, froze the samples, sliced them, and examined the samples under his microscope. To his surprise, the water samples exposed to positive words, phrases and music formed beautiful crystalline shapes. The negatively exposed samples formed dark and disorganized patterns. He concluded that since our bodies are composed of 75% water, it was also affected. Since the *'**Unihipili*** is the caretaker of the physical body, negative self-talk adversely effects both our emotional self and our physical body on a cellular level. Watch what you say and think to yourself.

3. The third technique is **APPRECIATION.** Practice the art of appreciation with your *'**Unihipili***. Express at every opportunity how much you appreciate what he or she does for you. Practice loving self-affirmation. Sincere phrases such as "I really enjoy being with you, " or "thanks for helping me with that," as well as "I love you" should be used often. Your inner self knows when you are being sincere, so don't try to pretend with it. (Your *'**Unihipili*** knows you better than anyone else in the world!)

The other part of this third technique is to set loving limits on what you do. When a situation arises that is questionable, such as taking that second piece of chocolate cake, or participating further in a relationship that isn't positive, say to your *'**Unihipili***, "I would like to think further about this before deciding what to do." (Remember the *'Uhane* is the decision-maker and needs to take its rightful place as the decision-maker of the team.) As you develop the ability to listen, voice your appreciation for your *'**Unihipili,*** and set loving limits, a most miraculous thing begins to happen. Your *'**Unihipili*** will present you with impressions through its other psychic senses. Most importantly your *'**Unihipili*** will send your prayers to the *'Aumakua* and pass on to your *'Uhane* the inspirations and creativity of your *'Aumakua*. The pathway to the *'Aumakua* opens up and you become a whole human being.

4. The fourth technique is **COUNTERING OLD HABITS**. Habits are patterns rooted in the *'**Unihipili*** that limit us, not only on the physical plane, but also on the spiritual plane. The *'**Unihipili*** stubbornly clings to what it possesses, whether it is a person, a thing or a belief. It resists change. In order to remain free and open to inspiration and creativity, we must be pliable and adaptable. Some habits, it may be argued, are good habits. However, we must be able to grow beyond our own limited beliefs of what is good for us at any given time. The ideal state is where the *'**Unihipili*** and the *'Uhane* accept the habit as a necessary selected personal discipline, but are able to release it when appropriate.

Whatever the habit, the first step in practicing this technique is to start with something simple.

For instance, if you normally eat only one thing at a time from your plate at meal times, consciously alternate portions. If you drive the same route to work, turn down a different street. If you plan your day down to the last minute, purposely under plan and leave time for play. Use your opposite hand more. Be aware of how you talk about people when they are not around. Practice saying only words you would say if that person were standing next to you. (Remember the beautiful crystalline forms of positive words and their effects on your body.) Use any activity that counters habits you have identified. Remember you are countering old habits and developing the trust to open to new possibilities.

5. The fifth technique is **CLEANSING**. Now is the time to begin the process of **clearing away** all the guilts, complexes and fixations that have taken root in your *'**Unihipili***. This is the job of the *'Uhane* as guide and teacher. This continuing process is crucial to the health and welfare of the Selves for these guilts, complexes and fixations block the path to the *'Aumakua*. There are many methods of accomplishing this cleansing. John Bainbridge recommends a method called "vectoring" in his book, *Huna Magic*, which helps identify the complex and gives specific techniques for clearing it away. Any method you choose will work, but the most critical part in any method is Love. The *'**Unihipili*** cannot be coerced into giving up its feelings of guilt. This only happens through love and forgiveness.

GUILT CAN ONLY BE CLEANSED AWAY THROUGH LOVE AND FORGIVENESS.

"Self-forgiveness" is a term used by many psychologists. It is in reality the forgiveness of the ***'Unihipili*** by the *'Uhane* and the forgiveness of the *'Uhane* by the ***'Unihipili***. True communication only comes through forgiveness.

Take some time right now to forgive yourselves repeating these words:

As the *'Uhane* to the *'Unihipili*: "I forgive you, unconditionally and sincerely, my dear Little Sister or Brother, for any and all hurts, whatever they have been. I truly love you. Will you forgive me for not listening...for not acting on your instincts and communications... for shutting you out... for not showing how much I really care about you... and for all the other hurts I have caused you? Will you please forgive me?

(Close your eyes and picture your two Selves embracing and feeling love for one another.)

Some complexes and fixations come from the deep, dark past. Only through love can you peel away the layers and discover the secrets and shadows hidden within and dissolve them with the light of love. Start on little things first. Develop trust through no judgment and reveal the guilt for what it really is -- a reaction to a person or situation. The *'**Unihipili*** made decisions based on incorrect information it received before the *'Uhane* became aware. Remember the *'Aumakua* is always ready to assist and help in this process. You only have to ask and your *'**Unihipili*** will contact the *'Aumakua* and request assistance for forgiveness.

The process of forgiveness is a cleansing process called *"kala"* in Hawai'ian. It is a very important principle of the ***Huna*** teachings. It is done on a daily basis in order to keep the Path between the *'Unihipili* and the *'Aumakua* clear. Long explains in *The Secret Science Behind Miracles,* that *"kala"* means to "cleanse ceremonially to remove guilt fixations which block the path." The root word *"Ka"* means to "radiate or reach between two places, and the root word *"la"* means "the Light." *"Kala"* also means, "to restore the light." The ancient *Kahuna* had a ritual that helped the ***'Unihipili*** clear away deeply rooted fixations, guilts and complexes. It is called the *Ho'oponopono* and you will find an explanation of this important ritual in a following section. (An example of a *Ho'oponopono Ceremony* is found in the Appendix.)

***KALA* SHOULD BE DONE EVERY DAY.**

INNERACTIVITY

Purpose: To teach the *'Unihipili* using the Will of the *'Uhane.*

THE BODY GAME

(Building Love and Trust)

Thinking engages the head and the brain. Feeling engages the trunk and internal organs. Willing engages the arms and legs. The realm of the ***'Unihipili*** is music, song, and symbols. We enter this realm to learn to do a sacred dance in this Inneractivity. Elaborate and purposeful movements require that you use the head and brains of your *'Uhane* and the arms and legs of your Will in coordination with the feelings of your trunk. Body movements to music require you to use all of these elements together.

1. Stand an arm's length distance from every other person in the group. Take a deep breath and quiet the mind and the body.

2. Keep your hands down at your sides, bend your knees slightly and move to your right first. Step right, left, right and then tap with your left foot. Keeping your weight on your right foot, now move towards your left. Step left, right, left and tap with your right foot, ending with your weight on your left foot. This completes the dance step. Practice a few times moving right and then left and back. (The count is right one, two, three, tap; left one, two, three, tap for a count of four in each direction.)

3. When you feel comfortable with the foot movements, add the arm movements. Extend your arms out to the side parallel to the floor as you do the steps. When you are moving right, extend the arms to the left. When you move to the left, change direction and extend your arms to the right. Practice the arms and feet movements together.

4. Now, put on some Hawai'ian music (or any Country/Western song that has 4/4 time or 4 counts to each measure) and move in time to the music. Start with slow music until you can do the steps and arm movements easily. Remember to keep the knees and the entire body relaxed. To sway the hips, bend the knees slightly.

5. When you can move the arms and legs together, try some variations. Move your fingers up and down in a wavelike motion as you extend your arms. (Congratulations! You are now doing the ***hula***!)

Start turning your feet in a circle, using the same one, two, three, tap dance step. Put your hands on your hips as you dance, or invent some movement that represents an element of nature or a feeling. How about expressing the movements of waves or wind? What would you do to represent the feeling of love? Add the movement of the fingers to these variations. (In the *hula*, women usually use a wavelike motion for the fingers and dance flowingly and gracefully. Men keep their fingers in a fist and dance with strength and boldness. Try both methods to get the feel of the different ways you can communicate with the hula.)

6. Use this dance exercise when you are feeling "out of sorts," having some difficulty in making a decision, or when you just want to have a moment of pleasure with your two Selves. Remember the ***hula*** originally was a sacred dance and you can use it in that context. The ***hula*** integrates both the *'Uhane* and the *'Unihipili* in a cooperative effort of expression. (And you get additional physical exercise when you dance.)

(Take a few minutes to write down anything that you want to remember about this **Inneractivity**. Was it easy to do the foot movements? Was it easy to do the arm movements? Did you have any difficulty in making the feet and arms move together in opposite directions? Was it easier to dance once the music was playing? Did you feel self-conscious when you tried to illustrate a feeling or element of nature?)

Personal Comments:

INNERACTIVITY

Purpose: To learn the name of your *'Unihipili.*

THE NAME GAME

1. Take out your pendulum. Explain to your *'Unihipili* that you want to learn his or her name so you can better communicate with each other. Explain that you are going to play a game that will help you learn the right name.

2. Explain and then show your *'Unihipili* that when the pendulum moves back and forth in a vertical motion, the movement means "yes." (Make the pendulum move back and forth as if you were nodding your head "yes.") Next explain and show the pendulum movement for "no," which is side to side in a horizontal motion. (Make the pendulum move side to side as if you were shaking your head "no.")

3. Ask your *'Unihipili* if it understands and if it will please make the pendulum move with its answer, either "yes" or "no?" If the answer is "no," or the pendulum isn't moving, go back to step 1, repeating the explanations until you get a "yes" answer. Don't worry if the movement of the pendulum is weak at first, it will become stronger as your *'Unihipili* learns to use it. You can also ask your *'Unihipili* to give you a stronger answer.

4. Now start asking about the name. Start with your own middle name. In childhood, we were often called by our full first and middle names, especially if we were in trouble. Ask, "Is your name (your middle name)?" Allow time for your *'Unihipili* to answer "yes" or "no" by moving the pendulum.

5. Keep trying other favorite names. Then try all other names that come to you. Don't be discouraged if you don't learn the name in this first practice. Remember the *'Unihipili* can be stubborn at times or might not feel trusting. (It took me a full year to learn the name of my *'Unihipili.*) If it gets tired of playing the Name Game, give it up for that session and try again later. Be persistent, however. By disclosing its name to you, your *'Unihipili* has taken the first big step in developing trust.

6. At the end of each session with the pendulum, remember to thank your *'Unihipili* for its cooperation and love. Praise yourself for doing a good job.

As soon as you learn the name of your *'Unihipili,* use it whenever you are talking to your *'Unihipili.* By using its name you are showing honor and respect and intimacy. Use this same method to discover the personal name of your *'Aumakua.*

(Take a few minutes to write down anything that you want to remember about this **Inneractivity**. Did your *'Unihipili* readily reveal its name? Did your Little Sister or Little Brother cooperate in using the pendulum for this **Inneractivity**? Did you become frustrated because the name did not come forth?)

Personal Comments:

CONTINUING INNERACTIVITY

Purpose: To continue to communicate with your *'Unihipili* using the pendulum.

Use the pendulum to communicate with your *'Unihipili* about other areas of your life. Use the same basic "yes" and "no" movements. You may find it helpful to add two other directions. These must be explained and demonstrated to your *'Unihipili* before you begin to use them. A circular motion clockwise represents "I don't want to tell you," and a circular motion counterclockwise represents "I don't know."

The *'Unihipili* can only answer questions that require a "yes" or "no" answer in this method. It cannot foretell the future because only the *'Aumakua* knows the future. If you do ask it questions about the future, it will give you answers it thinks you want to know. Remember it wants to please you and will take every opportunity to do so.

Using the pendulum is very helpful, but the best method is to develop and use the inner communication between the Selves.

Continuing Personal Comments:

THE *HUNA* PRAYER (THE *HA* RITE)

Prayer was a very important ritual for the ancient *Kahuna*. Prayer was a process of directing, not petitioning. Therein lies the power of the ***Huna*** Prayer. Through the research of Max Freedom Long, we have learned much about the making of a prayer according to the ancient *Kahuna*. The prayer is never rushed, but deliberately thought out in advance with all the ramifications of the answer considered as fully as possible. The prayer is carefully worded and imaged by the *'Uhane* and sent to the *'Aumakua* by the *'Unihipili* AS ALREADY IN THE DESIRED STATE (the pattern) with a surcharge of *mana* or energy to be used in answering the prayer.

REMEMBER, THE *'UNIHIPILI* IS THE ONE WITH THE DIRECT CONNECTION TO THE *'AUMAKUA* ALONG THE *AKA* CORD.

FAITH

All religions and beliefs teach that FAITH is an important element in prayer. The ancient *Kahuna* also taught that faith is important. You must believe that the process works and that the answers will come from your *'Aumakua*.

DESIRE

The other important element in prayer is DESIRE. Desire implies that your emotions are involved and so they should be, for it is the cooperation of both the emotions and the thoughts (or the *'Unihipili* and the *'Uhane*) that helps bring about the desired changes.

NO HURT

The third important element is NO HURT. The answer to the prayer must not hurt anyone or yourself. Long says "...it should be remembered that in all we do we are part of the world family, and anything that we ask that might take advantage of another member of the family, will probably get us no opening of the door of heaven when we knock."

The ancient *Kahuna* also taught that the only "sin" is hurt. There was no word in Hawai'ian for "sin." A new word had to be made up for the missionaries. This new word meant "excess baggage you keep carrying around with you." The missionaries taught that you could sin against God. The *Kahuna* taught that it was impossible to commit a sin against God, but you could hurt those around you, and this was the gravest error.

THE ONLY SIN IS HURT.

When you stop to think about the concept of "no hurt," you see it really is the basis for all other religious commandments. The Greek definition of "sin," according to Dr. Wingo, is "to shoot at a target and miss" or "to head toward a certain destination and go off the road." These definitions assume that the target can be hit with another try and the destination can be found by getting back on the right road. The ***Huna*** teachings agree with that definition. Hurting another person is indeed a grievous error that misses the mark, but you have another chance to set things right.

PRAYER IS A REQUEST FOR A CHANGE IN FUTURE CONDITIONS

All prayer is a request for a change in future conditions, whether it be a change in a physical condition that needs healing or a change in circumstances. The ancient *Kahuna* understood that the *'Aumakua* had the power to change the future. Since the *'Aumakua* was not allowed to interfere with the free will of the *'Uhane* and *'Unihipili,* it would answer any prayer sent to it in proper form. You are probably familiar with the phrase, "Be careful what you pray for, you just might get it!" In other words, your prayer must be carefully thought out or you might receive something you are not prepared to receive.

STEPS FOR MAKING AN EFFECTIVE PRAYER

The following steps, based on the research of Max Long and others are a good prayer method.

▲1. **Decide what it is you really want to change.** This is often the most difficult part of the prayer. Each prayer should have only one request for a change. Go through the prayer process separately for each change you desire. Be sure that you really want the change. Be willing to do your part if you get the change. For instance, if you want a new sports car, be willing to afford the payments, pay the insurance, pay for the upkeep and accept the responsibilities of driving such an expensive car. If you are requesting healing, be willing to do the things a healthy person does. If you want a new partner in your life, be willing to give of yourself in order to make the relationship work. Perhaps you really don't want a new sports car, but simply want a new car. Perhaps you really don't want a new husband or wife, but simply want a very good friend. Determining exactly what you want is often the hardest step in making a prayer.

> TAKE YOUR TIME TO DECIDE WHAT YOU REALLY WANT TO CHANGE.

It is also important to make sure that your *'Unihipili* wants to change what your *'Uhane* wants to change. Check with your *'Unihipili* using the pendulum method to verify that the new condition is really desired.

▲2. **Consider the possibilities of hurt.** Project yourself into the future and see what kinds of things might happen that could hurt you or someone else if you receive the change. Perhaps you desire the larger house next door. How will receiving the house next door affect the people already living in it? Will they experience a great hurt by losing their house? What about your own family? How will they be affected if you have to take a second job in order to pay a higher mortgage or rent? Will living in the house next door make you feel better or worse if you have higher utility bills to pay or a bigger yard to keep up?

> PROJECT YOURSELF INTO THE FUTURE.

▲3. Compose the words of the prayer. The wording of the prayer is very powerful. The *'Unihipili* takes words and sounds literally. Be careful that you have selected the words that convey the proper meaning and sound. Don't specify how the change will come to you. Use general terms. Allow the *'Aumakua* to do its part in generating the specifics with its greater abilities. Write down the words and work on the meaning and structure and sound of the prayer until you are satisfied that your *'Unihipili* understands exactly what you mean. Make sure you have covered all aspects of your requested change, including the means to pay for your request if it is a material item. You want the answer to the prayer to come easily and happily to you. You want the answer to be for the highest good of everyone involved. (Include this phrase in your prayer.) The words of your prayer will be spoken out loud bringing your Will or intention into action. Write down the final form of your prayer so that you can send exactly the same words each time you pray.

> **WORDS OF A PRAYER ARE VERY POWERFUL.**

▲4. Compose the images or pictures of the prayer. In addition to the words of the prayer, the images you send must also be carefully composed. Remember all prayer is telepathic and is sent as sensory images. The images are the perfect mold or pattern. They are not static but vibrant with energy. These images are often referred to as "holographic images" because they are not flat like movie images, but include the three dimensional aspects of sight, sound, touch, smell, taste and feeling. The images are the fully changed and perfect condition -- the end result. Put yourself in the pictures. Don't compose images of a sickly condition. In other words, picture a fully functioning leg, instead of a healed broken one. Picture the fully active leg in a perfect and healthy condition. See yourself running, jumping and using the leg as you would if it were healthy. Feel the healthy and active leg. This is also true for other conditions. If you are praying for financial changes, see yourself accepting a check, enjoying the plans you made to spend it, and the happy faces of all those involved with you. If you are praying for a new job, see yourself doing the activities of the new job, enjoying the companionship of your new colleagues, opening your pay envelope and seeing and feeling the new paycheck. Feel the sense of accomplishment.

> **PICTURE ONLY HEALTHY CONDITIONS.**

> **USE AS MANY OF YOUR SENSES AND EMOTIONS AS POSSIBLE IN YOUR IMAGING.**

Write down your specific holographic sensory images, so you can experience them exactly the same way each time you make the prayer. Include all the physical senses and emotions you can. For instance, if you are praying for money, feel the texture of the bills in your hands. Experience the feeling of happiness as you receive this money. See the happy expressions of the other people involved and hear their praises. Use as many of the five physical senses as you can and as many emotions as you can to form the experience of the perfect answer.

Most *'Unihipili* relate to the world in a visual manner. However, there are many that relate to the world in an auditory manner (with sound) and many that relate to the world in a kinesthetic manner (tactile). In reality we use all of our senses to relate to the world, but one sense is usually more predominant. Use whichever manner works best for you in the imaging, sounds and feelings of your prayer pictures and try to include as many of the other senses as you can. With practice you will become quite good at using all your senses and feelings.

Remember, when composing the prayer pictures use general terms rather than specifics. We are not able to see into the future and grasp the bigger picture. The *'Aumakua* will crystallize the future in the best way possible for you. There may be a better answer to your prayer than what you can see at the present. Be sure to use appropriate words and images to allow for this to happen. And don't forget to include a phrase such as "for my highest good and the highest good of all."

ALLOW THE *'AUMAKUA* TO DO ITS PART IN ANSWERING THE PRAYER

▲5. Do not change the words or images once you begin to pray. The *'Aumakua* wants to answer your prayer and give you every good thing it can. But if you change your mind and suddenly don't want what you originally prayed for, but want something else instead, you have changed the pattern for the answer. The *'Aumakua* cannot realize a pattern or request that is muddled or unclear. It will either wait until you have decided exactly what you want or you may receive a half-formed answer to your prayer. If you sincerely want to change the prayer, explain carefully to your *'Unihipili* to cancel the first prayer and ask its cooperation in sending the new prayer request. The first prayer must be canceled before you send the new prayer. Go through the steps again and spend more time deciding on what you really want.

DO NOT CHANGE THE WORDS OR PICTURES

▲6. Begin by making yourself deserving and place yourself in an attitude of reverence. To be deserving of the answer to your prayer you must be clear of all the hurts you have done to others. Spend some quiet time reflecting on your recent activities and those activities that have to do with your prayer request. If you sense any emotions around any of the activities, explore with your *'Unihipili* what these emotions are and whether there has been any hurt done to anyone. Has any hurt been done to any member of your family? Any hurts done to your friends? Any hurts done to strangers? Any hurts done to Mother Earth? If a hurt comes to your consciousness, you must make amends <u>before</u> the prayer will be answered. Often you can personally ask forgiveness of those you have hurt. If you cannot ask forgiveness personally, you can use other methods to make amends. For instance, you can make amends by giving to charity, either your money or your service. If there is no way you can make amends, you can ask that the Light of the *'Aumakua* be used to balance out the debt and fervently pledge to never make that mistake again. You may have to wait to finish the prayer process until the hurts have been amended to insure that the prayer has been sent.

MAKE YOURSELF DESERVING FIRST.

▲7. Enter into the Presence of your *'Aumakua*. Now is the time to enter into that Presence of the Divine. Light a candle or incense. Chant or use special words or music that call you to into the Presence. It is important to use some physical symbol to make this a sacred ritual. All of these actions impress your *'Unihipili*. Meditate on your *'Aumakua* and on the Oneness of all things. Use whatever method is most meaningful to you. You want your *'Unihipili* to know that this process is holy and sacred.

IN A STATE OF REVERENCE THE *AKA* CORD IS THE STRONGEST.

Use candles or music or meditation to alert your *'Unihipili* that you desire to make conscious contact with your *'Aumakua*. Picture this happening. Ask in a loving way for your *'Aumakua* to draw near and feel yourself in its holy presence. It is in this state of reverence that the *aka* cord between the *'Unihipili* and the *'Aumakua* is the strongest, because the *'Uhane* has taken its place as a conscious partner in the prayer process.

▲8. **Accumulate a surcharge of *mana*.** Accumulate a surcharge of *mana* using the method best suited to you. Long suggests that *mana* can be generated and stored by instructing the *'Unihipili* to begin the accumulation of *mana* and then breathing consciously in four sets of four breaths each. (The Ha Rite) The deep, deliberate breaths are accompanied by a visualization of the *mana* being generated and held ready to be sent with the prayer. Four sets of four breaths are usually enough, but if the problem is more difficult, accumulate more *mana*.

MANA IS ACCUMULATED BEFORE THE PRAYER IS SENT.

▲9. **While holding the *mana* in readiness, activate your Will and repeat the words of the prayer out loud followed by the holographic images. This should be done four times, remembering to hold the *mana* until the next step.** The *'Unihipili* knows how to send the prayer and often wants to send the *mana* off with the first recital. Encourage your *'Unihipili* to hold the *mana* until after the fourth recital so that the intention, words and pictures will be clear and strong.

▲10. **Send the words, images and *mana* to the *'Aumakua*.** After the last repetition of the words and images, instruct the *'Unihipili* to send the prayer, images and the *mana* to the *'Aumakua*. You may feel a change in your body as the prayer and the *mana* is sent. Some people feel this as a shudder or tingling, others as a feeling of relief. Still others feel nothing. Don't be discouraged if you feel nothing when the prayer is sent. You will become more sensitive to this process the more you use it. Have faith and believe the prayer has been sent.

THE WORDS, IMAGES AND ENERGY ARE SENT TOGETHER.

▲11. **If extra *mana* is needed, spend some time gathering and sending the extra *mana*, always holding the same image in your mind.** It is important not to change the image during this process. Generally this step is added if the need is greater, as for healing prayers.

REMEMBER TO OFFER *MANA* AND THANKSGIVING FOR YOUR BLESSINGS.

▲12. **Offer thanksgiving.** After the prayer has been sent with the words, images and the *mana*, it is time to thank your *'Unihipili* for its part in sending the prayer. Offer thanksgiving to your *'Aumakua* for its part in bringing the prayer into reality. **Remember this important step of thanksgiving!**

▲13. **Make a formal ending to the prayer.** It is important that you formally end the prayer so that the process is consciously finished. If your *'Unihipili* continues to send images and *mana* indiscriminately, the prayer may become muddled and confused. The ancient *Kahuna* used the phrase, ***"Amama ua noa. Lele wale akua la,"*** which means "The prayer has taken flight, let the rain of blessings fall." (Amen). As you end the prayer with an appropriate phrase, visualize yourself as being healthy, enjoying prosperity, feeling happy and filled with the joy of Service. Use the same picture of yourself at the end of each prayer. The effects of this visualization will be cumulative and you will find yourself experiencing all of these good things.

CONSCIOUSLY MAKE A FORMAL ENDING TO YOUR PRAYER.

▲14. Hold the faith that the prayer will be answered. Once you have planted the seeds of the prayer, know that they will grow into your answer. And don't worry or fret about the growing process. Have an expectant patience that the answer is coming into form. A gardener does not dig up his seeds to see if they are growing. The gardener plants them with the faith that they will grow, and grow they do, just as the gardener expects them to. And so shall your prayer grow into fruition. Avoid discussing your prayer with anyone who does not understand what you are doing or who will not support you. Their negative energy is not good for your faith.

HAVE PATIENCE AND YOUR PRAYER SEED WILL GROW.

▲15. Repeat the prayer process exactly as you have written and imaged it every day until the answer becomes reality. Depending on the difficulty of the request or desire and the amount of *mana* sent with the prayer to help with the realization, the number of days required to bring about the answer may vary. Some people receive instant answers. For others the answer needs time to crystallize. Two to three weeks is about average for most prayers to be answered, but the time can be shorter.

REPEAT THE PRAYER PROCESS EVERY DAY

▲16. Do your part. A person cannot be led to an answer unless he or she is moving along the path toward it. If you are praying for a new job answer ads, send out your resume, go on interviews. Do all the things necessary on this physical plane to accomplish the end result. If you are praying for healing, do what you know is necessary to speed the healing along. The *'Uhane* must continue to be a part of the team and do all that it can on the conscious level to help in the realization of the prayer.

TAKE YOUR RESPONSIBILITY AND DO YOUR PART.

The more you follow the prayer ritual, the more you open the *aka* connection to your *'Aumakua.* You may start to find that even small requests for changes or circumstances come almost immediately. Sometimes a careless phrase or a half-formed phrase will bring surprising results. Even spur-of-the-moment thoughts about something will bring it forth. When this begins to occur in your life, your *'Uhane* should remain alert so that stray words or thoughts are not sent by your *'Unihipili* into the realm of the *'Aumakua* or you may get what you <u>least</u> expect. Guard against hurrying the prayer process.

Remember the prayer process begins with a carefully and well-thought out <u>answer</u>, it doesn't begin with the <u>request</u>.

The ancient *Kahuna* used the symbol of the seed for the prayer. Within the seed is the pattern of the full-grown plant, an appropriate image for a prayer. Your images and pictures are the seeds you are planting in the fertile garden of the *'Aumakua*. Your *mana* is the rain that nourishes and helps the seed to grow.

"*Ano-ano*" means seed in Hawai'ian.

The Hawai'ian word for prayer is *"ano-ano,"* which has several meanings. By studying these meanings we can better understand the prayer process.

a. **A solemn stillness; a sacred place.** To make a prayer we enter into the silence or the holy place.

b. **An expression of certainty of something done or to be done.** The prayer is stated with certainty that it will be answered, the desired condition will come about.

c. **Now, at this present time, immediately.** The phrase used in most prayers is that the condition exists now, at this present time.

d. **Seeds, or seeds.** The prayers are like seeds that contain the pattern of the fully grown plant or idea.

e. **The meaning of a word or phrase. Likeness or image of a thing.** The prayers are carefully worded and the images or pictures are carefully formed to represent the words and ideas.

f. **The moral quality of an action, as good or evil, or the moral state of the heart.** Your prayer cannot hurt anyone or anything. The state of the heart of the sender is important to the process.

g. **To change or transform.** The prayer is sent as a request to change or transform the future condition.

h. **To change the external appearance.** The *'Aumakua* changes the external appearance, the physical form, of the condition.

i. **To set apart or consecrate for a special purpose.** The *'Uhane* and the *'Unihipili* consecrate the prayer action by charging it with love and *mana*.

THE HAWAI'IAN PRAYER METHOD

Max Long described the Hawai'ian method of making a prayer in his book, *Secret Science Behind Miracles,* based on his research of the root words of the following important phrases relating to prayer.

1. ***"Hoo-aka"*** means to "make very clear and properly understood." Prayer is serious business because one must be very careful to weigh all elements in the proposed prayer for a change in conditions, then picture the desired condition in careful and clear detail.

2. ***"Hoo-iha-iha"*** means "to cause the drawing tight of a rope," the ***Huna*** symbol of activating the *aka* cord that connects the *'Unihipili* with the *'Aumakua.* The secondary meaning is "to be intent" and this describes the state of mind of the *'Uhane* before making the actual prayer.

3. ***"Pu-le"*** means "to pray." *"Pu"* means "to come forth, as words from the mouth" also "to try to talk while holding water in the mouth" (holding energy). *"Le"* means "to leap or fly upward," the symbol of the thought-form picture of the desired changed condition passing along the *aka* cord to the *'Aumakua,* as well as the upward flowing of the *mana.*

4. ***"Hoo-mana"*** means "to cause superhuman power" and "to cause one to have regal authority." The prayer is presented at the symbolic altar sent to the High Place or *'Aumakua.* A sufficient amount of *mana* must be sent to allow the *'Aumakua* to break down the old future before it can arrive, and replace it with the new and desirable future condition. The *'Aumakua* transforms the *mana* so that it can make the desired changes. By giving the *mana* to the *'Aumakua* we are giving it regal or royal authority, giving the *'Aumakua* full authority to decide upon the good of granting or denying the answer to the prayer and the full authority to carry out the request in its own way.

5. ***"Mo-ahi-hoo-mana"*** means "to sacrifice by making *mana.*" A considerable time might be spent after delivering the prayer to "breathe life into it." A broken bone might need more *mana* than a request for intuition or guidance. Daily repetition of the prayer-action and the renewal of the supply of *mana* may be needed. The prayers are repeated four times word for word and image for image each time.

6. ***"Amama ua noa. Lele wale akua la,"*** means "The prayer takes flight. Let the rain of blessings fall." The formal ending of the prayer-action is critical. This is the invitation for the return flow of *mana* from the *'Aumakua,* whose purity can heal and bless. This establishes a complete circuit that does not deplete any of the Selves. The breaking of the contact at the ending of the prayer-action is important so that only the proper words and images are contained within the prayer.

THE *HA* RITE

The *Ha* Rite as suggested by Max Long is a structured ritual for sending the prayer. ("*Ha*" means "breath" and "four.") First, follow the steps outlined in The *Huna* Prayer method to compose the words and images to your prayer. When you are ready, ask your *'Unihipili* to contact your *'Aumakua* and move into the Presence.

Next, ask your *'Unihipili* to help you generate the *mana* to be sent with the prayer. The *mana* is generated in the *Ha* Rite by taking four sets of four deep breaths each. Remember to breathe naturally between the sets. Begin to breathe and gather the *mana*, but make sure your *'Unihipili* holds the energy until the prayer is ready to be sent.

When you have completed the 16 breaths, activate your Will or Intention and repeat the words of your prayer out loud in a strong and powerful voice. Follow the reciting of the words with the images you have composed. These images are to be strong, definite, colorful, and filled with all the good emotions you can generate. Spend some time picturing and feeling the answer to your prayer as a reality. Make sure you continue to hold the energy.

Repeat the words and pictures of your prayer four times. At the end of the last time, instruct your *'Unihipili* to release the *mana* and your prayer to your *'Aumakua.* Picture your prayer and the *mana* moving up and away from you and being received by your *'Aumakua.* Raise your arms and eyes upward towards the heavens as your prayer and *mana* are uplifted.

Make a formal ending to your prayer. Picture and feel the blessings of the *'Aumakua* returning to you as you stand in perfect health and happiness. Take a final deep cleansing breath and say "Amen" or "So Be It" or "And So It Is."

Resume your daily activities and keep the faith that your prayer will be answered – for it surely will!

THE PROCESS WORKS

If you have followed the prayer process exactly and kept your faith strong and have not received an answer within a reasonable amount of time, there may be something standing in the way of your prayer. **The process works!**

Consider the following suggestions if you have not yet received your answer:

1. **Go back over the steps to make and send a prayer.** Did you change the words or images of the original prayer? Sometimes subtle changes creep in when you are least expecting them. Compare the prayer you sent today with the prayer you sent on the first day. If the words or pictures have changed, you have probably not considered all the ramifications of the change you thought you wanted. If you need to change the prayer request, be sure to talk to your *'Unihipili* and make sure it cancels the first prayer and will cooperate in sending the new, revised prayer. This time

make doubly sure the answer, words and pictures are exactly the way you want them.

2. **More *mana* may be needed by the *'Aumakua* to fully answer the prayer**. A period of reasonable time may be different on the level of the *'Aumakua*. Perhaps a better answer to your prayer is coming and just needs more time to crystallize. Keep your faith strong and continue to send the prayer.

3. **Examine your faith.** Another common reason for a prayer not being answered is that you do not believe or have not held the faith that the answer will come. Perhaps you have begun to worry that nothing will happen. Be on guard. If you are feeling negative emotions about not receiving the answer to your prayer, and have voiced such thoughts and generated *mana* from such emotional negativity, the *'Unihipili* may send this negative idea as a new prayer and you will get exactly what you have been praying for - the negative. Bring all your positive resources to the front, so that any negative thoughts or feelings will be quickly neutralized and not sent as an additional prayer. Hold onto the positive, keep your faith that the prayer will be answered for your highest good, and continue sending the prayer.

4. **Confirm cooperation.** The next question to ask yourself is, "Did I get the full cooperation of my *'Unihipili* before we sent the prayer?" In other words, was the *'Unihipili* enthusiastic and willing to pray for the answer **and** did you check to make sure your *'Unihipili* wanted the answer as much as you did before you made the prayer? Was your *'Unihipili* willing to cooperate and did it cooperate in sending the prayer? (It is always wise to check with your *'Unihipili* in advance before making the prayer to make sure you have its full cooperation. Use your pendulum to double-check any unsure answers.)

5. **Sometimes the *'Unihipili* does not feel deserving of receiving such good things as those being requested.** Perhaps there is a guilt complex hidden deep inside that makes the *'Unihipili* feel undeserving of such a gift. This is most often the case. When the *'Unihipili* does not feel deserving or is feeling guilty about something that is connected to the request, it will **not** send the prayer. Often you have not cleared away the hurts done to others and the *'Unihipili* will not send the prayer because it is feeling guilty about having wronged someone. You, as the *'Uhane,* may assume the prayer has been sent, but in actuality the *'Unihipili* has not done its part. (Remember it can be quite stubborn at times.) Work with your *'Unihipili* to get to the root of the problem and use logic and love to dissolve away the guilt and help the *'Unihipili* feel more deserving. This is the reason for doing the *kala* process every day. To keep the path clear between the *'Unihipili* and the *'Aumakua,* all the obstacles must continually be cleared or cleansed away.

6. **The answer to your prayer might not be for your highest good.** There may be something better coming for you than you have been able to envision at the present time. In your prayer process you have given the *'Aumakua* the authority to answer the prayer in the best possible way for your highest good. Many people have reported that what they thought they wanted when they made the prayer was not nearly as good as what they actually received later. Keep the faith that your *'Aumakua* has a greater knowledge of your good and wants to give you only the best.

THE PROCESS WORKS!

INNERACTIVITY

Purpose: To compose a daily prayer of blessing to offer *mana* to your *'Aumakua.*

One of the easiest ways to remember to send a gift of *mana* to your *'Aumakua* on a daily basis is to add it to your mealtime blessing. As you bless the food, offer thanksgiving to your *'Aumakua* and send a gift of *mana.* Using the prayer steps outlined in the above section, compose a prayer to your *'Aumakua,* which you can use daily. A good quick phrase to remember in making a prayer is "ask, picture and give thanks." These elements should always be included in your prayer. Carefully select the proper words that are meaningful to both your *'Uhane* and to your *'Unihipili.*

Next, carefully select an image that represents or symbolizes the offering of your gift to the *'Aumakua* and write down key words or complete sentences to remind yourself of the correct image you want to send in the prayer.

Get ready to send your prayer. Reverently request that your *'Unihipili* contact your *'Aumakua* and ask that it be present. Accumulate a surcharge of *mana* and send the prayer. Formally end your prayer. After the prayer has been sent, thank your *'Unihipili* for doing its part in sending the gift of *mana* to your *'Aumakua.* Thank your *'Aumakua* for its blessings.

Write the words to your prayer here:

Write the images to your prayer here:

(Take a few minutes to write down anything that you want to remember about this **Inneractivity**. Was your *'Unihipili* willing to work with you to form a prayer of blessing? Did you find it easy to hold the *mana* until after the appropriate time to send it? Did you feel the presence of your *'Aumakua* at any time during the prayer process?)

Personal Comments:

ALTERNATE GROUP INNERACTIVITY

Use this **Inneractivity** for a group. Follow the steps outlined above for making a prayer. Members of the group suggest the words and images and all the *'Uhane* and *'Unihipili* present agree on them before accumulating the *mana* and sending the prayer. This prayer could be composed for world peace, enlightenment, healing, prosperity, etc. Write down the words and images so that everyone can see them.

Form a circle, holding hands. A linked circle is particularly appropriate when offering a group prayer. Direct the *aka* cords towards the center of the circle and weave them together to contain and transmit the highly charged *mana* and the prayer request. Ask the *'Aumakua* of all those in the group to be present for the prayer before beginning the accumulation of the *mana*. Use the *Ha* Rite of four sets of four breaths each. One person should lead this, counting the breaths for the group. Be sure to remind the *'Unihipili* to hold all of the *mana* until the prayer is read and imaged by the group. Repeat the words and images four times.

Then raise your eyes and joined hands towards the Heavens and send the *mana* and the prayer to the Po'*e 'Aumakua*. Wait an appropriate length of time before formally ending the prayer so that all the *mana* can be sent. Offer thanks for the assistance of all the *'Uhane*, *'Unihipili* and the *'Aumakua* gathered there for their participation in making and answering the prayer. Formally end the prayer ritual and close the circle with linked arms for a group embrace.

Write the words to the group prayer here:

Write the images to the group prayer here:

(Take a few minutes to write down anything that you want to remember about this **Inneractivity**. Was it easier or more difficult to compose a prayer with a group? Could you feel the increased *mana* as it was being gathered and held? How did it feel to raise your eyes and arms to pray rather than fold your hands and lower your eyes? Did you feel the presence of the *Po'e 'Aumakua*?)

Personal Comments:

THE HOʻOPONOPONO CEREMONY

The ***Hoʻoponopono*** was a special group or family ceremony performed when a person had difficulty in removing a guilt, complex or fixation from his or her *ʻUnihipili.* A *Kahuna,* who had been consulted in the matter, directed the ceremony of the ***Hoʻoponopono***. The *Kahuna* talked extensively with the person needing help and also with the person's family. Usually the problem was with another member of the family. The ancient *Kahuna* used whatever beliefs the person held true to construct a potent ceremony for impressing his or her *ʻUnihipili*. (The process works, no matter the words or the beliefs.) This ritual usually contained a powerful element that was symbolic of cleansing or washing away the old guilts or wrongs.

If a troubled person held Christian beliefs, then those beliefs were used to communicate with the *ʻUnihipili*. The person was directed to confess the sin, then to fast and give money or service to the church until it hurt, and do enough penance to cleanse away the sin and be forgiven. Often Holy Water would be used as a symbol in the cleansing ritual.

If a troubled person was a Hawaiʻian, who believed in the outer religious teachings, those beliefs were used. For example, the Hawaiʻian would be directed to eat only certain foods, wash in a specific lagoon, and offer sacrifices to certain gods in order to be cleansed and healed.

Whatever the rituals of penance and cleansing, or the amount of sacrifice required, the *ʻUnihipili* had to feel that it was doing <u>enough</u> to be cleansed of the wrong it had done and would be forgiven. If amends could be made with the person wronged, the troubled person was required to personally make amends and ask for and receive forgiveness. If this was not possible, then some other form of making amends was used such as those suggested previously. Sometimes the *'Aumakua* was asked to bring its Light and balance out the wrong doings and thus cleanse the *ʻUnihipili.*

The practice of doing penance to receive forgiveness is found in most religions and mystical teachings. The ***Huna*** teachings explain why this practice is so important. The path between the *ʻUnihipili* and the *'Aumakua* must be kept clear of all guilt, fixations and negative complexes. These act like blocks or obstacles or knots in the connection. When the path is blocked there is no clear communication between the physical Selves and the Spiritual Self. The *ʻUnihipili* cannot fully contact the *'Aumakua* and deliver the prayer and *mana*. Nor can the *'Aumakua* fully contact the *ʻUnihipili.* Nor can the *ʻUhane* receive the energy, inspiration and intuition it needs to function.

THE *HUNA* TEACHINGS EXPLAIN WHY FORGIVENESS IS SO IMPORTANT.

It is the all important duty of the *ʻUhane*, as guide and teacher, to help the *ʻUnihipili* search out the hidden guilts, fixations and complexes lodged within and help the *ʻUnihipili* to let go of them and feel cleansed, healed, forgiven and loved. The more you are able to clear, the more trust your *ʻUnihipili* will have in your *ʻUhane*, and the more garbage will come up to clear away. It's a continuing process, but one that **must** be done. Only in this way can you become the whole human being you are meant to be.

CLEANSING THE GUILTS IS A CONTINUOUS PROCESS.

Long talked of the *'Unihipili* keeping "a little bag of secret guilts." These are taken out when the *'Unihipili* is bored and it relives these episodes over and over, often as dreams. Our nightmares come out of these "little black bags" of personal troubles. Our *'Unihipili* has gathered these secret guilts over the years. They are usually feelings of shame and unworthiness that were lodged early in our development, when we had to rely on others to help us make our moral decisions. The guilt or fixation or complex is generally associated with a particular age in our development. Discussing a specific age with our *'Unihipili* can sometimes lead to uncovering these secret guilts. Remember the *'Unihipili* will hide its head in shame from the *'Aumakua* if it is feeling unworthy because of guilt. There is no time like the present to begin to uncover and remove these from our lives.

NOW IS THE TIME TO BEGIN TO CLEAR AWAY THE GUILTS.

INNERACTIVITY

Purpose: To clear away the guilts, complexes and fixations lodged in the *'Unihipili* so the pathway to the *'Aumakua* will become clear.

(The following **Inneractivities** are based on exercises by Enid Hoffman.)

Find a quiet place where you can work undisturbed for about 30 minutes. Relax your mind and your body. Take four deep breaths and ask your *'Unihipili* to just start thinking about something, anything at all, it would like to bring to the attention of your *'Uhane*. Let the thoughts flow wherever they will. Let your *'Unihipili* control the thoughts and memories that enter into your center of consciousness. (This is opposite to what you do when meditating when you want to quiet your thoughts.) Don't resist the flow, just let the memories and thoughts come without making any judgment of their importance. When you feel a twinge of emotion accompanying a thought explore and feel that emotion. It's okay if tears fall.

When the memories or thoughts start repeating, engage the perspective of your *'Uhane* and gently and lovingly thank your *'Unihipili* for presenting them. Ask in a quiet and non-threatening way about those particular memories to help the two of you understand what happened to make them such strong memories. Ask if there is any need for *kala* regarding them. Remember not to judge, for your *'Unihipili* has already judged the actions and feels guilty. Simply help cleanse away the negative feelings and reassure your *'Unihipili* that he or she is worthy and loved and can release whatever has been held concerning these memories.

When the session is over, give yourself a big hug and say, "I love you." (Actually wrap your arms around your body.) Go to the nearest mirror and look yourself straight in the eyes and repeat "I love you." This is an excellent **Inneractivity** to use regularly to pinpoint those guilts that need cleansing away. Sometimes you will receive happy memories that both Selves can enjoy.

(Take a few minutes to write down anything that you want to remember about this **Inneractivity**. Was it easy to hug yourself? Could you feel the love from your *'Uhane*? Did your *'Unihipili* cooperate by sharing some memories with you?)

Personal Comments:

CONTINUING INNERACTIVITY

Purpose: To continue the process of *kala*, the clearing of the path between the *'Unihipili* and the *'Aumakua*.

Keep a **Notebook of Unfinished Business**. Use the same method as described above, but ask your *'Unihipili* to bring to your center of attention a person with whom you have unfinished business. Your *'Unihipili* will know to whom you are referring. Write the person's name at the top of a blank page in your notebook. Then ask your *'Unihipili* to tell you the nature of the unfinished business it feels you have with this person. Listen quietly and record any words, impressions or feelings the *'Unihipili* sends you about the person. Again make no judgments, but simply record the information. Thank your *'Unihipili* for sharing with you and ask it to let you know of any other unfinished business with that person during the next week. Then end the session. Be sure to write down this information when it is presented during the week. When one week has passed, open the notebook and review what has been written there. Consult your *'Unihipili* on the best way to resolve or clear up this unfinished business.

When the two of you have agreed on a resolution, take action. Perhaps you can call that person and ask forgiveness. It is critically important that you take the action necessary to finish the business with each person. When it is complete, go on to another person and repeat this process. The clearing up of unfinished business is an effective way to clear away obstacles from your path.

Continuing Personal Comments:

OBSESSIONS, POSSESSIONS, AND UNWANTED OUTSIDE INFLUENCES - EATING COMPANIONS

Throughout the history of the world we find firm evidence that outside influences, beyond our normal range of perception, do affect us. Both psychic scientists and psychiatrists agree that people can and do become obsessed or even possessed by outside spirits or influences. Many religions teach about discarnate spirits that try to affect the living. The Christian *Bible* states that Jesus cast out "demons" or "evil spirits." The Roman Catholic Church practices exorcism. The ancient Hawai'ian believed that we are often influenced by the spirits of the dead. They believed that the spirits of their ancestors were in communication with them and could be called on for help in times of trouble. They also believed that there were other disembodied spirits they could contact that would work for good or for evil. They could also contact nature spirits or group spirits.

Sometimes the two Selves or consciousnesses of both the *'Uhane* and the *'Unihipili* are torn or yanked out of the physical body due to a sudden or unexpected death, such as an automobile accident. The connecting *aka* cord to the physical body is unexpectedly severed. This disconnected spirit is called in Hawai'ian "*a kino wai lua,*" meaning "a body of two waters." The body (*kino*) being the *aka* body and the two waters being the two kinds of *mana* related to the two Selves.

With this unexpected severing, the two Selves become lost and disoriented. They may wander around the spiritual plane looking for their physical body without success. They are unaware that they have died to the physical world. They reach out for any life force they can find and sometimes take it from the living. If the path to their *'Aumakua* has been blocked during their lifetime, these wandering souls are cut off from their Higher Self that has the power to help them. This combined *'Uhane /'Unihipili* spirit soon learns how to exert hypnotic control over another living person and force their negative, and sometimes evil emotions and desires, on that person. In some cases, the combined spirits may possess the living person and force the rightful *'Uhane* out of the body. In other cases, both rightful Selves are forced out and the living person takes on a totally new personality, usually ending up committed to a mental hospital as insane. In fact, obsession insanity afflicts the majority of those in mental institutions.

Some living people are only slightly obsessed by a *'Uhane/'Unihipili* spirit and these people can function normally, except when the outside spirits generate the emotional explosions and strange unaccountable fears. These disconnected spirits are called "Eating Companions" in Hawai'i, meaning that they partake of the energy or vital force of the living person.

Both the *'Uhane* and the *'Unihipili* can also become lost from each other and wander around separately trying to take *mana* from the *'Unihipili* of the living. Without a *'Uhane*, a *'Unihipili* cannot reason and cannot find its way. It begins to steal vital force from the living. It often becomes a poltergeist, feeding on the strong emotional energies of a fearful young person. A *'Unihipili* who learns to steal *mana* from the living can even manifest a ghostly form. It can take possession of a person as a "secondary personality." It can also drain all of the vital force from a living person causing complete exhaustion or even death.

Without an *'Unihipili*, a wandering *'Uhane* is weak but also feeds on the vital force energy of living people. It cannot remember anything and searches for an *'Unihipili* and its memories. Most often an *'Uhane* is too weak to obsess or possess a living person on its own, but it does have the power to influence thoughts and actions of a living person in strange and negative ways.

LEGENDS IN HAWAI'I

In ancient Hawai'i there are legends and stories of people dying willingly and separating their *'Uhane* and *'Unihipili* from the *kino*, in order to protect a sacred place, such as a temple, in spirit form. There are also stories of evil *Kahuna* trapping disconnected *'Unihipili* and *'Uhane,* and using their trained hypnotic power, cause the discarnate spirits to destroy the living through a death prayer. In older days in Hawai'i if someone felt greatly wronged, he or she could go to one of these *Kahuna* and ask for help in punishing the wrong doer. If the *Kahuna* felt the action justified, he would then instruct his captured spirits to seek out the wrong doer and begin the *mana* draining process. These spirits had been taught to find the *Kahuna's* victim and suck all of the life energy away causing death. As late as 1958 there were hospital reports of people who were being prayed to death. No modern medical treatment could prevent the draining of the person's life force in these cases and the people died. The vital force was drained away from the feet first, making them numb. The numbness traveled up the body until the numbness reached the heart, at which time the person died of heart failure.

There were ways, however, in which a victim could countermand such an action. If the person strongly believed he or she was innocent, the death prayer would have no effect. Or the person could engage the services of another *Kahuna*, who could turn the spirits back on the sending *Kahuna*. Sometimes this meant death to the sending *Kahuna*, if he had not adequately protected himself. When a person believed he or she was being prayed to death, he or she could also go directly to the sending *Kahuna,* make amends, ask forgiveness of the person wronged, and do a great penance. The sending *Kahuna* would then call off the evil spirits and all would be well.

Sometimes outside influences are relatives who have passed on, but are still clinging to a member of the family. Sometimes, spirits calling themselves Spirit Guides or Angels attach, but both kinds of spirits are still draining energy from the living. We have given them permission at some time to become attached. It is better to be in alignment with these outside spirits than to have them attached. Check with your *'Aumakua* through your *'Unihipili* whether the Spirit Guides or the Angels are actually from the Higher Spirit Realm and working for your highest good. If they are not willing to become unattached, they need to be removed.

THE HUNA TEACHINGS GIVE US THE KNOWLEDGE OF HOW TO PROTECT OURSELVES

How does the knowledge of the ancient *Kahuna* concerning disconnected spirits affect us today? We accept the fact that there are things happening on other levels we don't understand. Our best modern psychologists and psychiatrists cannot explain the workings of the human mind or how we come to be obsessed or possessed. By understanding and using the ***Huna*** model and the knowledge of the ancient *Kahuna* we can learn how to protect ourselves from any kind of outside influence from whatever source it comes.

How do we know we are being affected by outside influences? Most of the time we are not aware that any spirits or outside influences are hanging around us. We may, however, be aware that sometimes we react in an abnormal way to certain situations. We find ourselves exhibiting erratic behavior. We might feel we are being drained of physical energy. We might feel something is going on at our "gut level," but we are unable to distinguish or interpret what that might be. Or we might just feel "out of sorts." If you become aware of any of these feelings, it is possible that a disconnected spirit is hovering around trying to take some *mana* from you. Your *'Unihipili*, if it trusts you, will confirm to you whether any outside influences are around. You can use the pendulum to check. Don't panic if the answer is "yes." There are ways to handle these problems.

TECHNIQUES FOR KEEPING OURSELVES CLEAR

It important to clear away anything that is draining your *mana* without your permission. In order to maintain optimum physical health and to keep any obsessing, possessing, unwanted outside influences, or eating companions away, use the following techniques:

1. Begin at once to **"clean your house"** by discovering and cleansing the hidden guilts, complexes or fixations of your own *'Unihipili.* Develop a trusting and loving relationship between the two Selves, so that your *'Unihipili* will tell you immediately if any outside influence is trying to affect you.

2. **Practice good constantly**. If you happen to do or say something that hurts another, ask for forgiveness at once and make appropriate amends. Doing a good deed every day goes a long way towards living the proper life. Random acts of kindness and love help to keep clear the path to your *'Aumakua,* and keep negative influences away.

3. **Bless everyone and everything**. Bless those that seem to harm you in thought, word or deed. Radiating the positive energy of love will turn any negative influences away from you. Maintain an attitude of positive thinking and acting.

4. **Ask your *'Aumakua* for help** in clearing away and keeping away any obsessing, possessing or unwanted outside influences. Include in your daily prayer a request that you are surrounded and shielded by the **Protective Light of the Divine**.

INNERACTIVITY

Purpose: To check with your '*Unihipili* for unwanted outside influences and send a Prayer of Protection to your '*Aumakua*.

(Based on the work of Rev. James Venable Alexander)

Find a quiet spot where you won't be disturbed. Take out your pendulum and ask your '*Unihipili* to cooperate with you in determining whether you are being affected by any outside influences. Ask the following questions:

1. Are any disconnected obsessing or possessing influences, spirits or entities attached to us now?

2. Did any disconnected, obsessing or possessing influences, spirits or entities tell you to tell me "no" when the answer is really "yes?"

3. Is this something born to me in this lifetime that is interfering with my life?

4. If it wasn't in there now, was it in there before?

5. Is it still attached to me?

6. Is this for my highest good?

7. Can we get rid of it?

8. Will you contact the '*Aumakua* and ask for help in getting rid of it?

After you have finished asking your questions and have determined that you need to clear away any outside influences, build a surcharge of *mana* and repeat the following prayer (or one of your own making) with **strong** conviction and power:

PRAYER OF PROTECTION

Beloved '*Aumakua*, through my Companion Self (use the name of your '*Unihipili*), we pray to you now. We pray that any and all spirits or outside influences of any kind that were not born into this body in this lifetime and that are not for our highest good are cast out now! We pray that all spirits or outside influences of any kind that we knowingly or unknowingly have previously given permission to be present in us be cast out now! We revoke that permission now and ask that they be cast out! **Now, now, now,** never to return to us again in any way, shape, type or form. We pray that these spirits or outside influences be sent back to their source, never to return to us. We pray that they are sent back now.

Send the Light of your Power and Love to surround and protect us and to fill us up casting out any and all dark influences.

(Imagine a brilliant White Light from your *'Aumakua* coming towards your body until it surrounds you completely, including over the top of your head and underneath your feet. This White Light interpenetrates your body until you glow with the Divine Light of your *'Aumakua*, casting out any shadows, darkness or attachments and filling those places with White Light.)

(Repeat the prayer and the visualization four times and then release the *mana* and the prayer.)

We give thanks, Beloved *'Aumakua* that this prayer has been answered and we are now, and will continue to be, filled with your Light and Love. *Amama ua noa. Lele wale Akua la*. Our prayer has taken flight. May the rain of blessings fall. And so it is! Amen.

(Take a few minutes to write down anything that you want to remember about this **Inneractivity**. Did you feel afraid when we talked about disconnected spirits? Was your *'Unihipili* cooperative in telling you the answers to the questions? How did you feel after the Prayer? Was it easy to see the White Light all around you?)

Personal Comments:

HEALING AND THE USE OF *MANA* IN HEALING

All healing comes from the *'Aumakua* of the individual or the *Po'e 'Aumakua* of all the people involved in the healing process. Healing is a change of a future condition. Healing **always** involves a prayer. It may not be a formal prayer, but any wish, desire or intention directed towards healing is automatically sent by the *'Unihipili* as a prayer. Many people have been miraculously healed as they prayed, for they were in a highly charged emotional state (vitalized with *mana*). This kind of healing is attributed to the remarkable "power of prayer." These prayers are answered because they were unconsciously sent with an extra surcharge of *mana*. Most people don't know that energy must be sent with a prayer and usually receive little or no change in their condition.

Instances of miraculous healings have been recorded around the world, including Hawai'i. Perhaps the most miraculous kind of healing to Western thinking was the *Kahuna's* ability to bring the dead back to life. Sometimes the *'Aumakua* would place *mana-loa* in a sacred stone or in a sacred place and people would place their hands on the stones and pray to be healed. The *mana-loa* would then be transferred into their bodies to produce the healed condition. There are many such sacred places found around the world where *mana-loa* is active and causes healings that are not explained by current medical science. Lourdes in France is one of these places, where the *mana-loa* is found in the healing waters. The henges of England are other sites of healing.

The ancient *Kahuna* used *mana*, together with strong suggestions and a physical stimulus, to affect healing. The physical stimulus impressed the *'Unihipili* of the patient and strengthened its belief that the healing process would work. The medicinal plants they prescribed, as well as the specific rituals, are examples of physical stimuli that impressed the *'Unihipili*. The power of the *Kahuna's mana* was used to firmly plant the suggestion of healing in the patient's *'Unihipili*. *Mana* or vital force was also used directly on the physical body to stimulate the healing of a specific part.

THE PROCESS OF HEALING

The process of healing is described as follows: from the healer's *'Unihipili* to his or her own *'Aumakua*, using the *'Uhane*'s intention or Will for healing, the prayer and the *mana* are first transferred to the patient's *'Aumakua*. The patient's own *'Aumakua* dissolves the unhealthy condition in the *kino*. Then using the pattern or mold of the perfect *aka* body of its *'Unihipili*, it utilizes the *mana-loa* to construct the healthy condition and place it back into the *kino* causing the healing.

No matter the outward appearance of the healing ritual, this is the process. No person can claim responsibility for doing the healing. The healing comes from the *'Aumakua* of the patient needing the healing. The healer's *'Aumakua* takes part in the healing, but it is the patient's *'Aumakua* who directs the healing. Healing prayers should always include a request that the healing be for the highest good or highest purpose of the patient. In some instances, physical or emotional healing is not in the best interest of the patient, nor does it serve a higher purpose. It is up to the patient's own *'Aumakua* to make this decision.

PSYCHOLOGY IS AN IMPORTANT PART OF THE HEALING PROCESS

Psychology was always a critical part of the healing arts for the *Kahuna*. They taught that unhappiness and physical illnesses are directly related. They first carefully questioned anyone who came to them for healing to determine if there was some unhappiness involved. They used their extensive knowledge of psychology to facilitate the healing of the *'Unihipili*, which in turn facilitated the healing of the *kino*. They worked to clear the path to the *'Aumakua* so the prayer and *mana* for healing could be sent. They also believed that if a person changed his or her thinking about a troubling matter, the circumstances would invariably change and the person would be healed.

Modern psychology is based on uncovering hidden problems in the subconscious mind. When these problems are brought to light and understood, many negative physical conditions heal. Through *Huna* we understand that the subconscious mind is the *'Unihipili*. The *'Unihipili* manifests physical conditions in an effort to get the attention of the *'Uhane* to help solve or get rid of emotional problems. If the *'Uhane* is not paying attention, the *'Unihipili* "steps up the heat" and causes more negative physical conditions until the *'Uhane* has no choice except to stop and listen. A good resource for discovering hidden problems correlated to specific physical conditions is *You Can Heal Your Life* by Louise Hay.

USING *HUNA* TO HEAL OURSELVES

We are expected to request healing for ourselves!

Healing can take the form of physical changes, mental changes or changes in one's circumstances. The process is always the same. The *'Aumakua* dissolves the future and reconstructs it according to the plan sent by the *'Uhane* and the *'Unihipili*. Sufficient *mana* must be sent to the *'Aumakua* to be used to form the answer. This request is sent as a formal prayer or as a request for assistance in a healing process. Prior to any healing of others or our selves, the all important step of forgiveness must be accomplished. The *'Unihipili* must feel worthy to send the prayer and receive the blessings of the prayer.

FORGIVENESS MUST BE ACCOMPLISHED FIRST FOR THE HEALING PROCESS TO BEGIN.

When the *'Uhane* takes its rightful place in the human trinity, it rightfully follows that we must practice healing in our own lives and in the lives of those around us. The practice of ***Huna*** is the practice of healing. It is the healing of our body, our conditions and our circumstances. As Long puts it, "if you are not using ***Huna***, you are working too hard."

HEALING OUR CIRCUMSTANCES

You can use the *Huna* teachings to heal or change your circumstances. Healing circumstances comes after much thought and the methodical projection of your self into the future, where you can consider all aspects of the change. Do this by activating your imagination with the cooperation of your *'Unihipili*. It is not a quick fix process. **(Remember, be careful what you pray for, you just might get it!)**

In ***Huna*** the most important consideration of any change in circumstances is whether or not the change or healing will hurt anyone or your self. If you are facing a situation where change could possibly hurt both you and another person, your responsibility is to your own self. For instance, if a change in circumstances means you need to leave a relationship that isn't right for you, but your leaving will hurt the other person, you must choose your own *'Unihipili* over the other person. Your Selves are ultimately more important to you than the Selves of any other person. And this is how it is meant to be. Your *'Uhane*, *'Unihipili* and *'Aumakua* are always your first priority. However, if you find yourself in this kind of situation, you can choose to do everything possible to minimize the hurt to the other person.

There are those people who have progressed to the point of complete agreement between the three Selves about loving and selfless service. They have chosen to put others ahead of themselves, dedicating their lives to a higher purpose. These enlightened beings are well advanced upon the Path and choose the life of service consciously and with the blessings of the P'oe *'Aumakua*. Most of us have not reached that level of consciousness yet. We are on that level, however, where we can consciously practice the helpful and hurtless life.

HEALING MENTAL AND EMOTIONAL ATTITUDES

Changes in our mental and emotional attitudes come about through diligent work with our *'Uhane* and *'Unihipili* to root out old attitudes and replace them with new productive attitudes. When impasses occur, you can request assistance from your *'Aumakua*, who stands ready to help at all times. Changes in mental and emotional attitudes are fairly easy changes to make. Positive affirmations, carefully worded and spoken by the *'Uhane* are powerful tools to affect changes in our attitudes. Affirmations are really a type of hypnotic suggestion made to the *'Unihipili*. When affirmations are used for a certain period of time they can reprogram negative attitudes. Changes in mental and emotional attitudes change your life. ***Huna*** teaches that the most effective affirmations or suggestions are those given with a surcharge of *mana*. This powerful reinforcement of energy sets the affirmation in the *aka* body of the *'Unihipili* and helps to neutralize more quickly the negative aspects and influences of the old mental or emotional attitude.

CHANGES IN MENTAL AND EMOTIONAL ATTITUDES CAN CHANGE LIVES.

Remember emotions follow thought. Use positive words with the desired condition already established. An example of this would be NOT - "...every day in every way I am getting better," BUT - "Every day I am perfect in every way."

THE LANGUAGE OF THE *'UNIHIPILI* IS EMOTIONAL AND SYMBOLIC.

Along with the words, picture the desired changed condition. The language of the *'Unihipili* is totally symbolic and it understands the pictures more than the words. The words of an affirmation repeated out loud with a charge of *mana* are more firmly placed in the *aka* body of the *'Unihipili* when they are accompanied by a strong, positive image.

Repeat your affirmation at the same time every day for at least 21 days to firmly establish the new attitude. After the affirmations have been carefully worded, gather a surcharge of *mana* by breathing deeply a few times. Then engage the Will or Intention of the *'Uhane* and speak the words aloud with conviction. At the end of each statement, picture the desired changed condition. Repeat the statements and visualizations four times, exactly as you have them written and visualized. After the fourth repetition,

AFFIRMATIONS SHOULD BE SAID WITH A SURCHARGE OF *MANA*.

mentally direct the *mana* and the statements towards the *'Unihipili* to be stored in the *aka* library. The *'Unihipili* will search for similar memories and store the new memories with the old ones. As the new mental and emotional attitudes become stronger memories through repetition, the old memories will weaken and be replaced.

HEALING THE *KINO*

One of the greatest skills we can acquire is the skill to diagnose and affect healing in our own bodies. Often we are not even aware of what is going on in our bodies. We hold on to stress, sometimes the stress of a job we don't like, sometimes the stress of a bad relationship, sometimes the stress of not being able to do what we really believe we should be doing. This stress lodges in our bodies and we don't know how to release it. Stress is only a symptom of illness. It is really the result of an inner conflict between the *'Unihipili* and the *'Uhane*.

Dr. John Diamond, in his book, *Life Energy*, tells how our emotional attitudes affect our health. He states that "everything we have inhaled, eaten, done or not done, thought or not thought over all the years of our lives culminates in illness." He states that we all have the power to learn how to find the precise emotional attitude that is causing a specific physical or mental problem. He suggests we can learn to identify and recognize the emotional attitude, cease to dwell on it, give it up, and transmute it with the power of affirmative words. He calls this "psychobiological harmony." We call it ***Huna***.

OUR EMOTIONAL ATTITUDES EFFECT OUR HEALTH.

This is the same process the ***Huna*** teachings suggest in ridding the *'Unihipili* of guilts, fixations and complexes. Dr. Diamond explains that we must assume the responsibility for ourselves and use our Will power to maintain a positive balance in our lives. ***Huna*** teaches us that we can train our *'Uhane* to take its rightful place as guide and teacher, using the Will to infuse purpose and meaning into our lives and to create the kind of future that we want for health and happiness.

OUR WILL INFUSES PURPOSE AND MEANING INTO OUR LIVES.

Dr. Diamond suggests that stress allows negative emotional patterns to be established. When these set in different parts of our bodies, they build up until an unhealthy physical condition appears. As we understand through the ***Huna*** teachings, this stress is caused by the conflict between the *'Uhane* and the *'Unihipili*. When the conflicts are resolved and released, the stress disappears and the body reflects a healthy condition. He also suggests that we activate our life energy when both sides of our brain or the cerebral hemispheres are balanced. When they are balanced we can reach our life's goal of life energy, positive health, harmony, creativity, effective communication and insight.

STRESS IS CAUSED BY THE CONFLICT BETWEEN THE *'UHANE* AND THE *'UNIHIPILI*.

In ***Huna*** we understand that he is referring to the balance and cooperation of the *'Uhane* and the *'Unihipili.* There is a point in the physical brain and the interpenetrating *aka* bodies of the two Selves where they interface. It is the point of conscious communication where the talents of each Self come into play creating a powerful new ability to relate to life. This point can only be opened and the power tapped when there is cooperation, love and trust between the Selves. This is one of our goals in practicing the ***Huna*** teachings.

In Dr. Diamond's book, he explains how to use muscle testing to determine the underlying emotional attitudes. He also explains that the thymus gland, located just beneath the upper part of the breast bone in the middle of the chest, is the gland that controls the life energy (*mana*). The thymus plays an important role in the body's immune system. It monitors and regulates the life energy flowing through the body's energy systems. It is the link between the energy of the mind and body (*'Uhane* and *'Unihipili*). It can initiate instantaneous corrections to rebalance a body that is out of harmony. Through the thymus we activate our Will to Wellness.

ACTIVATING THE THYMUS BEFORE STARTING ANY WORK WITH THE *'UNIHIPILI* PROMOTES BETTER HEALTH

It is helpful to activate the thymus gland before starting any work with the *'Unihipili.* Gently tap the area where the thymus is located. This stimulation not only gets the attention of your *'Unihipili*, but also activates your Will to Wellness and increases the flow of *mana* to your body. The *mana* then flows to that part of your body that is out of balance.

You, as the *'Uhane*, can help to maintain your own physical health by "Cleaning House," ridding yourself of negative mental and emotional attitudes, and by daily activating the flow of *mana* to your physical body. Your *'Unihipili* will then do its part in keeping you healthy.

INNERACTIVITY

Purpose: To activate the thymus and begin the affirmation process to bring about optimum health.

(This **Inneractivity** is based upon the work of Dr. Diamond.)

1. Lie on your back on the floor or other hard surface with your knees raised and your feet slightly apart so that your thighs are in alignment with your shoulders. You can use a small pillow or stack of books to elevate your head to a comfortable position.

2. Accumulate a surcharge of *mana* by the breath method and ask your *'Unihipili* to store the *mana* until you direct where it should go.

3. Activate your thymus gland by gently tapping the thymus area on your chest.

4. Repeat the following affirmations slowly and with conviction. After each affirmation, tap your thymus area again.

♥ I am Love and I am loving.

♥ I have faith and trust, gratitude and courage.

♥ I am humble, tolerant and modest.

♥ I am happy, cheerful and have good fortune.

♥ I reach out with love and kindness to everyone and everything.

♥ I am secure and have confidence in my future.

♥ My sexual energies are in balance.

♥ I am clean and good and worthy of being loved.

♥ I renounce the past and live fully in the present.

♥ I am generous.

♥ I am relaxed.

♥ I forgive and I am forgiven.

♥ I am content and tranquil.

♥ I am filled with hope and light.

♥ I am alive with joy.

♥ I am in harmony and peace.

♥ I am Love and I am loving.

5. At the end of the affirmations, repeat the following prayer:

"Thank you my dear Little Sister or Little Brother for your love and assistance. Thank you dear *'Aumakua* for your love and assistance. I am now filled with the power and energy of Love and Light. I remain in a perfect state of Love and Light."

6. Open your arms with your palms up and release the *mana* to go to the *'Unihipili* for the balancing of the body and to the *'Aumakua* as a gift and end the exercise with the words, "And so it is."

(Take a few minutes to write down anything that you want to remember about this **Inneractivity**. Did you notice any sensations in a specific part of your body as you repeated the affirmations? Were there any affirmations you had trouble saying with conviction? What was the feeling in your body when you finished the **Inneractivity**?)

Personal Comments:

CONTINUING INNERACTIVITY

Purpose: To practice a more powerful method for keeping the body healthy.

Following the steps outlined above, go through the affirmations three times. The first time use the word "I," which has the awareness that the *'Unihipili* is speaking. The second time use the word "You," which has the awareness that the *'Uhane* is speaking. The third time use your first name, which has the awareness that the *'Aumakua* is speaking. If you know the name of your *'Unihipili*, use the combination of your names the third time. Use the three different awarenesses to bring harmony and more power to the health process. Release the *mana* and thank your other Selves before formally ending the **Inneractivity**.

Continuing Personal Comments:

THE IDEAL HUMAN

"When the personality comes fully to serve the energy of its soul, that is authentic empowerment," says Gary Zukav in his book, *Seat of the Soul*. The ***Huna*** teachings say the Ideal Human is that state in which the *'Uhane*, *'Unihipili* and *'Aumakua* are all working together sharing the Divine energy, each doing its part to insure health, success and happiness. It is "the human/divine trinity living as one."

As you integrate your three Selves and fully energize your *kino*, you become more conscious of your true being. As you incorporate and use the talents and gifts of your three Selves, you gain a new sense of unity within and with all other beings.

Max Long states in his book, *Mana, or Vital Force*:

> In your approach to *Huna* you will, perhaps for the first time, come to see clearly that you, as a being of three closely related spirits, must try to remain aware of the obligations on each of these three levels of life represented by three levels of consciousness." [A person must]..."function and grow on and through and into all three levels.

Many philosophers and great teachers over the centuries refer to this state as "waking up" or gaining "awareness." The more you use the *Huna* teachings the more you awaken the cells in your body to its true reality. The more you follow the *Huna* path of service and no hurt, the more the Divine Light from your *'Aumakua* enters the consciousness of your other Selves. You become an illumined or awakened Soul.

The ancient *Kahuna* taught patience about life. They believed that every living thing was exactly in its intended stage of development or evolution. They taught that there is sufficient time for all of us to grow upward. And so we must take our own time to learn, to explore and to become proficient in using the abilities and talents of each of our Selves to become the Ideal Human. We grow into that state in which we evolve and expand to our fullest potential and beyond. For as the *'Uhane* learns love, compassion, wisdom, clarity and truth and the *'Unihipili* learns discipline, responsibility, discernment and compassion, the path to the *'Aumakua* is fully opened and we are finally able to realize our full power as a human being. Becoming an Ideal Human is not about our relationship with others, but our relationship with **Our Selves**.

The Ideal Human is the pattern of our true being. It is the goal, the attitude, the vision of what we are to become. The Ideal Human is a fully integrated awakened being living in awareness that every thought, word and deed is divine and is meant to express the divine qualities of Love, Peace and Light.

You have the power to become an Ideal Human. Use the teachings and tools in this book to discover the gifts and talents of your inner Selves. Keep the connection to your Higher Self, your *'Aumakua*, open and strong. Invite your *'Aumakua* to be a vital part of your life. Express Love and Gratitude to your Higher Self on a daily basis. Love and appreciate your Little Sister or Brother, your *'Unihipili*. Set the intention of your Older Brother or Sister to guide and direct you in the higher path of Love in all things. Take care of and energize your *kino* so that your physical vehicle is strong and healthy. As you pray, breathe in the Divine Light every moment and reflect it back to the world. Breathe out Divine Love to every being.

Give thanks that you are now fully awakened to your true nature. You are the Ideal Human expressing the sacredness of all life.

CLOSING PRAYER FOR GUIDANCE

Through our beloved *'Unihipili*, to our Divine Mother-Father-God, our Beloved *'Aumakua*, we ask that Divine Order, Unconditional Love, Radiant Health, Unending Wisdom, Unlimited Abundance, and Joyful Happiness be manifested in our lives right now. We see ourselves as expressing these gifts to all beings and in all circumstances. We give thanks that your Divine Light illuminates and guides us, as we come into a fuller understanding of the creative power we have within us to shape the future towards a better world. Let your Light and Love shine through us and through all Beings.

***Amama ua noa. Lele wale akua la.* Our prayer has taken flight. May the rain of blessings fall on all that are gathered here. And so it is. Amen.**

BIBLIOGRAPHY

Adams, Ansel. *An Introduction to Hawaii,* San Francisco, California. 5 Associates, Inc., 1964.

Alexander, James Venable. "Huna 101 Workshop" presented to members of Cape Girardeau Huna Fellowship, Cape Girardeau, Missouri, AudioTape. Huna Research Inc., 1997.

Bainbridge, John. *Huna Magic.* Los Angeles, California. Barnhart Press, 1988 & 1994.

"Biography of Franz Anton Mesmer-Founder of Mesmerism." http://easyweb.easynet.co.us/dylanwod/morganic/bio_mesmer.html.

Borysenko, Joan and Joan Drescher. *On Wings of Light: Meditations for Awakening to The Source.* New York, New York. Warner Books Inc., 1992.

Bray, David Kaonohiokala and Douglas Low. *The Kahuna Religion of Hawaii.* Borderland Sciences Research Foundation, Inc., 1990.

Carruthers, Martyn. *Human Consciousness and Decision Making,* (keynote talk to University Forum on Human Consciousness). http://www.spiritual.org. June, 1997.

Carruthers, Martyn. *Huna, Healing and Ohana.* http://www.spiritual.org. Martyn, 1998. Carruthers@Compuserve.com, 1998.

Churchward, James. *The Lost Continent of Mu.* New York, New York. Paperback Library, 1968.

Daws, Gavan and Ed Sheehan. *The Hawaiians.* New York, New York. Walker & Company, 1970.

Diamond, John, M.D. *Life Energy.* New York, New York. Dood, Mead & Company, Inc., 1985.

Dudley, Michael Kioni. *Man, Gods, and Nature.* Honolulu, Hawaii. Na Kane O Ka Malo Press, 1990.

Emoto, Masaru. "Die Botschaft des Wassers," *ZeitenSchrift,* Germany. February, 2000.

Ferguson, Marilyn. *The Brain Revolution, the Frontiers of Mind.* New York, New York. Taplinger Publishing Co., 1973.

Ferson, Baron Eugene. "The Star Exercise." http://www.sartek.com/Power/Starx.html.

Glover, William. *Huna, the Ancient Religion of Positive Thinking.* Cape Girardeau, Missouri. Huna Press, 1983.

Hay, Louise L. *You Can Heal Your Life.* Carson, California. Hay House Inc., 1984 & 1987.

Hernacki, Mike. *The Ultimate Secret to Getting Absolutely Everything you Want.* New York, New York. Berkley Publishing Group, 1988.

Hill, Napoleon. *Success Through a Positive Mental Attitude.* New York, New York. Simon & Schuster, Inc., 1960 &1977.

Hitchcock, H. R. *An English-Hawaiian Dictionary.* Rutland, Vermont. Charles E. Tuttle Co., 1887 & 1968.

Hoffman, Enid. *Huna, a Beginner's Guide.* Rockport, Massachusetts. Para Research, Inc., 1976.

Jones, Thomas, Editor. *The Hawaii Book.* Chicago, Illinois. J.G. Ferguson Publishing Company, 1961.

Kramer, Penelope. "In the Flow: A Conversation with Mihaly Csikszentmihalyi." *Intuition Magazine.* August 1996.

King, Serge. *Kahuna Healing, Holistic Health and Healing Practices of Polynesia.* Wheaton, Illinois. The Theosophical Publishing House, 1983.

Koran, Al. *How to Bring Out the Magic in Your Mind.* New York, New York. Frederich Fell, Inc., 1985.

Lee, Pali Jae and Koko Willis. *Tales From the Night Rainbow.* Honolulu, Hawaii. Night Rainbow Publishing Co., 1986 & 1984.

Lewis, Allan P. *Living in Harmony Through Kahuna Wisdom.* Las Vegas, Nevada. Homana Publications, 1984.

Long, Max Freedom. *The Huna Code in Religions.* Santa Monica, California. DeVorss & Company, 1965.

Long, Max Freedom, *Introduction to Huna.* Cottonwood, Arizona. Esoteric Publications, 1975 Reprint.

Long, Max Freedom, *Mana and Vital Force.* Cape Girardeau, Missouri. Huna Research, Inc., 1978.

Long, Max Freedom, *Psychometric Analysis.* Santa Monica, California. DeVorss & Company, 1959.

Long, Max Freedom, *Short Talks on Huna.* Cape Girardeau, Missouri. Huna Press, 1978.

Long, Max Freedom, *The Secret Science Behind Miracles.* Marina del Rey, California. DeVorss & Company, 1948 & 1954.

Long, Max Freedom, *The Secret Science at Work.* Marina del Rey, California. De Vorss & Company, 1953 & 1984

Long, Max Freedom, *How to become a Magician.* http://ourword.compuserv.com/homepages/hunahq/, 1988.

McBride, L.R. *The Kahuna Mystics of Old Hawaii.* Hilo, Hawaii. Petroglyph Press, 1972 & 11th Printing 1990.

Millman, Dan. *Sacred Journey of the Peaceful Warrior.* Tiburon, California. H.J. Kramer, Inc., 1991.

Morgan, Dylan, "What Mesmer Believed." The Journal of the National Council for Psychotherapists and Hypontherapy Register. Summer, 1994.

Northrup, Christiane, Dr. *Women's Bodies, Women's Wisdom: Creating Physical and Emotional Health and Healing.* Bantam Books, 1998.

Parfitt, Will. *The Elements of Psychosynthesis.* Great Britain. Element Books, 1990.

Powell, A.E. *The Etheric Double, the Health Aura of Man.* Wheaton, Illinois. TheTheosophical Publishing House, 1925 & 1979.

Pukui, Mary and Samuel H. Elbert. *New Pocket Hawaiian Dictionary.* Honolulu, Hawaii.University of Hawaii Press, 1975 & 1992

Redfield, James. *The Celestine Prophecy.* New York, New York. Warner Books, Inc., 1993.

Schuster, Donald H. *Huna, a Magic Way of Life.* Ames, Iowa. Research Into Mind, 1992.

Steiger, Brad. *Kahuna Magic.* West Chester, Pennsylvania. Whitford Press, 1971.

Thurston, Mark. *Paradox of Power.* Virginia Beach, Virginia. A.R.E. Press, 1987.

Wallace, Robert. *Hawaii.* Alexandria, Virginia. Time-Life Books, Inc., 1973.

Waters. G. T. *Follow Your Path.* Dallas, Texas. Arize, Inc., 1986.

Wilkerson, Dr. Clark. *Hawaiian Magic.* Whittier, California. Stockton Trade Press, 1968.

Wingo, Dr. Otha. *The Huna Way To Effective Living.* A Lecture Series Given to The Oklahoma Metaphysical Society, Audiotape, Cape Girardeau, Missouri. Huna Research, Inc., 1997.

Wingo, Dr. Otha. *Light-Switch Huna.* http://ourword.compuserv.com/homepages/hunahq/,1988.

Wingo, Dr. Otha. *The Story of the Huna Work.* Huna Research, Inc., 1995.

__________, *Huna Psychology: An Introduction*
http://ourword.compuserv.com/homepages/hunahq/.1988

Zukav, Gary. *Seat of the Soul.* New York, New York. Simon & Schuster, 1989.

APPENDIX

HO'OPONOPONO CEREMONY

A Cleansing Ceremony of Forgiveness

***Ka Noonoo Nui Ana*:** (Minister/Leader)

We invite you to be in an attitude of silence, quiet meditation, in preparation for this Hoʻoponopono, a Cleansing Ceremony of Forgiveness.

***Pule 'Aumakua*: Prayer for Inviting the Presence of our Higher Selves.** (Minister/Leader)

We offer this prayer to the *Po'e Aumakua*, the High Selves, of our *ʻOhana*, our family gathered here. We offer this prayer with the full and willing cooperation and agreement of our minds and our hearts, our *ʻUhane* and *ʻUnihipili.*

Beloved *'Aumakua*, Divine Mother-Father-God, we pray that you be present with us now. We implore your help to cleanse away all the past hurts and offenses we have done to others. Be present with us now. Help us remove these blocks from our Paths that we may experience your Light in our lives. Be present with us now. Amen.

***Ha La*: Breath of Light** (Congregation/ʻOhana together)

(Take four deep breaths and hold the energy, the *mana.*)

***Pule Wai A 'Aila*: Prayer to Bless the Water and Oil** (Minister/Leader)

Po'e 'Aumakua, we ask your blessings on this water (pour a little into the bowl) that it might be transformed into *Wai Hemolele*, Holy Water, to cleanse, purify and release us, offender and offended. Let it cleanse away forever all of the unwanted and negative memories that have blocked our path to you, our Higher Selves.

Po'e 'Aumakua we ask your blessings on this oil (hold up container) that it might be transformed into *'Aila Hemolel*e, Holy Oil, that will mark us as forgiven in your grace. Amen. And it is so! (Release the mana to the *Po'e 'Aumakua.*)

***Ha La*: Breath of Light** (Congregation/ʻOhana)

(Take four deep breaths and hold the *mana.*)

***Pule Ke Kala Ana Iho*: Prayer of Self-Forgiveness** (Congregation/ʻOhana)

From the awareness of the mind, repeat these words with great conviction:

My dearest *ʻUnihipili*, my beloved Little Sister (Little Brother), I unconditionally and sincerely forgive you now for any and all hurts, whatever they have been, whenever they occurred. I truly love you. I FORGIVE YOU NOW!

Response: (Congregation/ʻOhana)

Yes, I forgive you!

Will you forgive me for not listening, for not acting on your instincts and communications, for shutting you out, for not showing how much I really care about you, and for all the other hurts I have caused you? PLEASE FORGIVE ME NOW.

Responsive: (Congregation/ʻOhana)

Yes, I forgive you!

(Direct the *mana* towards your Inner Self and release it.)

***Ha La*: Breath of Light** (Congregation/ʻOhana)

(Take four deep breaths and hold the *mana*.)

***Pule Kala:* Prayer for Forgiveness.** (Congregation/ʻOhana)

Divine *'Aumakua*, if we, our families, relatives, and ancestors have offended any individual, family, relative or ancestor in thoughts, words or actions, from the beginning of our creation to the present....HUMBLY, HUMBLY, we ask you for forgiveness for all our errors, resentments, guilts, hatreds, hurts, traumas, pains, offenses, unkind thoughts, words or deeds, which we have created and accumulated from the beginning to the present, PLEASE FORGIVE US! PLEASE FORGIVE US! PLEASE FORGIVE US!

Response: (Congregation/ʻOhana)

YOU ARE FORGIVEN!

If we, our families, relatives and ancestors have held on to any offending thoughts, words or actions, from the beginning of our creation to the present, done to us by any individuals, families, relatives or ancestors...HUMBLY, HUMBLY, we ask you to forgive us for feeling offended and for clinging to and reliving such offenses, and for all the desires for vengeance, revenge, or hurts we have imagined, spoken or taken action towards, from the beginning to the present, **PLEASE FORGIVE US! PLEASE FORGIVE US! PLEASE FORGIVE US!**

Response: (Congregation/ʻOhana)

YOU ARE FORGIVEN!

(Release the *mana* to your *'Aumakua.*)

Ha la: **Breath of Light** (Congregation/ʻOhana)

(Take four deep breaths and hold thc *mana.*)

Pule Kii: **Prayer of Imaging** (Minister/Leader)

Close your eyes and open your hands as you visualize and feel a great Orb of Golden Light coming from your Higher Self, your *'Aumakua,* to rest in your hands. It is time to pull out all the hurts, offenses and negative memories you have uncovered and give them to your *'Aumakua.* Picture them flowing out of your body into the Orb of Golden Light. The Orb has an infinite capacity to absorb all that you can give. Keep pulling out the hurts and letting them flow into the Orb until every cell in your physical body and every cell in your mind, heart and spiritual bodies are clear and pulsating with Light. (Pause) When your body is completely filled with Light, release the Orb of Golden Light back to your *'Aumakua,* who will transmute the Orb and its contents into loving energy. See and feel the Orb of Golden Light lifting from your hands, rising to the Heavens and being received by your Higher Self.

(Release the Orb and release the *mana* to your *'Aumakua.*)

Ka Hana Kala: **Thc Ritual of Clcansing.** (Minister/Leader)

We invite you now to come forward to ritually cleanse yourself of all obstructions or blocks by washing your hands in the Holy Water, the *Wai Hemolele*, and receiving the mark of forgiveness with the Holy Oil, *'Aila Hemolele.*

(Each participant comes forward one at a time and a small amount of water is poured into his or her hands, which are washed and dried. Participants then kneel, sit or stand to receive the mark or forgiveness.)

(Minister/Leader administers the mark of forgiveness saying:)

Ke Keiki a 'Ohana La, Child of the Family of Light, receive this Holy Oil as a sign that you have been cleansed and forgiven. (Make mark on forward and then place hands on top of head and on heart.) The Power of the Light blesses you. In the name of that Sacred Spirit, whom you hold most dear, you are forgiven! Rise and go in peace.

(When everyone has washed their hands and received the blessing, cover the water and oil with a cloth.)

Ha La: **Breath of Light.** (Congregation/ʻOhana)

(Take four deep breaths and hold the *mana.*)

He Olelo Hooia: **Affirmations of Forgiveness** (Congregation/ʻOhana)

I am now ready and willing to receive the perfecting presence of the *'Aumakua* in my life.

I am now thankful for the mercy, joy and love that this life has bestowed upon me.

I have now forgiven myself for every thought, word, and deed I have embraced or undertaken that has kept me from the realization of the Truth about myself and the perfect unfolding of the Divine Plan for my life.

I have now forgiven everyone for every thought, word, and deed they have embraced or undertaken that has kept them from the realization of the Truth about themselves and me, and the perfect unfolding of the Divine Plan for our lives.

I have forgiven all! I release all! I am now free from all, except the perfect and Divine Plan and purpose for my life!

For this, I am so very grateful! And so it is! (Release the *mana* to your *'Aumakua.*)

Ha La: **Breath of Light** (Congregation/ʻOhana)

(Take four breaths and hold the *mana.*)

Pule Ho'ola: **Prayer of Healing** (Minister/Leader)

(All stand and raise eyes to the Heavens and lift up arms for the final prayer.)

Beloved *'Aumakua*, we thank you for this healing of forgiveness. Let Divine Order, Light, Love, Peace, Balance, Understanding, Joy, Abundance and Wisdom be manifest for us now. We are whole and perfect. May your Spirit proceed us in every act, thought and deed from this moment forward as we live the hurtless and loving life in service to humanity. In your name and in the names of the *Po'e 'Aumakua*, we know that it is done. And so it is! (Release the *mana* to the *Po'e 'Aumakua.*)

Amama ua noa. Lele wale Akua la. Our prayer has taken flight. Let the rain of blessings fall. Amen.

(The Congregation/*ʻOhana* joins hands and forming a circle sings an appropriate song, such as "The Peace Song" to formally end the ceremony.)

This ceremony is based on the writings of Iyanala, James Alexander, and Morrnah N. Simeona. Any part may be modified to meet the needs of the participants.

GLOSSARY

Aka – An etheric substance that connects everything in the universe; a container. It conducts energy and can be attached and stretched out like threads.

Ano-ano – Seed, more specifically the seed prayer.

'Aumakua – The Higher Self, your Guardian Angel, the superconscious mind, the "utterly trustworthy parental spirit."

Ha – Breath or the number four.

Ha Rite – Method of gathering energy by breathing four sets of four breaths each developed by Max Freedom Long.

Hawai'i—The name given to the islands in the middle of the South Pacific.

Ho'oponopono – The act of forgiving and making right, especially a forgiveness ceremony.

Hula – The traditional Hawaiian sacred dance.

Huna – The Hawaiian word that means "secret" adopted by Max Freedom Long to designate the inner teachings of the ancient priest.

Kala – Cleansing, the process of clearing away guilts and hurts, especially daily cleansing.

Kahuna – The Hawaiian priest, the "keeper, guardian or transmitter of the secret."

Kino – The physical body.

Kumulipo – The Hawaiian Chant of Creation that follows the evolution of creation.

La – Light.

Mana – The energy that permeates the universe, especially the energy of the *'Unihipili*, the subconscious mind and the body.

Mana-mana – The mental energy of the *'Uhane*, the conscious mind.

Mana-loa – The creative energy of the Higher Self, the *'Aumakua*.

Po'e 'Aumakua – The greater company of *'Aumakua.*

Pule – A directed prayer offered with the face uplifted and eyes open to the heavens which is sent with *mana.*

'Uhane – The conscious mind, the Older Brother or Sister Spirit.

'Unihipili – The subconscious mind, the Younger Brother or Sister Spirit.

HUNA PRAYER

BY

Max Freedom Long

If I have hurt someone today
With thought or word or deed
Or failed another in his need,
I now repent.

If I can take those steps again,
Tomorrow will I make amends
And heal with Love those hurts.
I do this pledge.

And if a hurt has struck me deep
And no amends are made,
I ask the Light to balance all.
I count the debt as paid.

Parental Spirits, whom I love
And who I know love me,
Reach through the door I open wide.
Make clear my Path to thee.

(Max Long suggests that you breathe deeply, concentrate the mana and visualize when you say this prayer.)

Also by Arlyn J. Macdonald

BOOKS

Parenting for Heart, Mind and Spirit
How to Effectively Parent Your Child, Your Self, and the Greater Community of Life
(available at buybooksontheweb.com and bookstores everywhere)

Nurturing Our Inner Selves
A Huna Approach to Wholeness
(available at buybooksontheweb.com and bookstores everywhere)

BOOKLETS

GETTING TO KNOW YOU!
An Introduction to Your Subconscious Self

THE GUIDE
Your Conscious Self

INDWELLING SPIRIT
Your Higher Self

EFFECTIVE HUNA PRAYER

THE HUNA BIRTHING BOOK

(Booklets available at huna.us)

LaVergne, TN USA
14 December 2009
166983LV00002B/99/A

9 780741 413734